How to Market Your Business

An Introduction to Tools and Tactics For Marketing Your Business

by
Ian B. Rosengarten, MS, MPH

Small Business Sourcebooks
from
Sourcebooks, Inc.
Naperville, Illinois

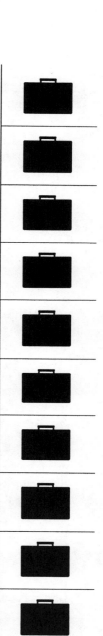

Published by: **Sourcebooks Trade**
A Division of Sourcebooks, Inc.
P.O. Box 372, Naperville, Illinois, 60566
(708) 961-2161
FAX: 708-961-2168

Cover Design: Wayne Johnson/Dominique Raccah
Interior Design and Production: The Print Group

This publication is designed to provide accurate and authoritative information in regard to the subject matter covered. It is sold with the understanding that the publisher is not engaged in rendering legal, accounting, or other professional service. If legal advice or other expert assistance is required, the services of a competent professional person should be sought.
From a Declaration of Principles Jointly Adopted by a Committee of the American Bar Association and a Committee of Publishers and Associations

The **Small Business Sourcebooks** series is designed to <u>help you teach yourself</u> the business essentials you need to be successful. All books in the series are available for bulk sales. Feel free to call us for information or a catalog. Other books in the series include:
- *How To Get A Loan or Line of Credit*
- *Your First Business Plan*
- *Smart Hiring for Your Business*

Library of Congress Cataloging-in-Publication Data

Rosengarten, Ian B. , 1950-
    How to market your business / Ian B. Rosengarten.
        p.   cm. -- (Small business sourcebooks)
        ISBN 0-942061-45-4 (pbk.) : $8.95. -- ISBN 0-942061-48-9 (hard) :
    $17.95
        1. Marketing--Management. 2. Small business--Management.
    I. Title. II. Series.
    HF5415.13. R64   1993
    658.8--dc20   92-41062
                                                                                CIP

Printed and bound in the United States of America.
Hardcover--10 9 8 7 6 5 4 3 2 1
Paperback--10 9 8 7 6 5 4 3 2 1

Acknowledgments

To Maxine for the opportunity; to Beth for the idea; to Kate with love for her support; and to Mona for help along the way.

Table of Contents

An Introduction

About This Book

Marketing is a fact of life, and fortunately there are many options available. The perfect combination of strategies for your particular situation and budget can be designed with a little creativity and some judicious planning. That's where this book comes in. *How to Market Your Business* has a place in your library as a general resource. It was written to provide you with ideas and concepts that you can refer to frequently when contemplating new marketing strategies or evaluating old ones.

General and specific marketing tools are listed in alphabetical order in the encyclopedia that follows. Each entry has a set of symbols to give you an idea of the time, planning and cost that may be involved, an explanation of how the tool works, and suggestions on how it might be used in marketing your business.

Rather than turn you loose at this point to read through the encyclopedia, which might quickly overwhelm you, we have put together a system to get you going as quickly as possible.

The first part of the book deals with marketing terms and concepts, and how you can apply them to your business. In many cases you'll also be given specific examples. That is followed by the marketing tools themselves which are all alphabetized and cross-referenced for your convenience.

However you decide to use this book, we hope it will provide you with many marketing ideas, save you time, energy and even money when you use it.

What is Marketing?

Marketing is the distribution, promotion and direction of products or services to your consumers. Simply said, marketing is everything you do to promote your business.

This includes a wide range of activities—from selecting the name of your business, to finding its location, to implementing an advertising campaign, to interacting with clients/customers, and more. Marketing, as a man-made science, is imprecise. What works at one time, won't necessarily work at another, and a message that sells to one person, may not work with another. Some efforts have probabilities attached to them—a direct mail campaign can be designed based on general assumptions using marketing industry information about what's worked and what hasn't from past experiences. Other efforts are difficult to assess. How do you know that your expensive stationery or packaging are making a difference? These difficult-to-assess items require a big dose of faith, especially when it's time to pay the invoices they may generate. To create a successful business, all small business owners must have an organized plan for getting the word out—that they exist, that their service/product is needed, and that what they sell is reasonably priced and readily available.

The Marketing Mix

The Product, Price, Place & Promotion

Commonly referred to as the "Four P's," the marketing mix is the foundation of marketing theory.

Product—The first P is the product or service you offer. The philosophy involved in selling goods is finding out the *needs* of the target consumers, whereas the underlying idea in providing services, is finding out what *problems* need to be addressed.

Price—The second P is price. This includes price determination, pricing policies and specific pricing strategies. The pricing of goods is based on actual costs, demand and competitive constraints. The prices of goods are easily compared and discounted. Service pricing is based on the personal benefit or value the consumer derives.

Place—Or distribution is the third P. The marketing channel of distribution is any business or individual who facilitates the flow of goods and services as they move from a producer to the actual user. This involves any intermediaries such as agents and brokers, as well as wholesalers. Service providers look towards "gate keepers" such as referral sources to channel business in their direction. Distribution is more applicable to goods than to services.

Promotion—The final P in the marketing mix. Here, products and services are promoted to sell. Before you are ready to promote your product, it needs to be packaged, which includes developing a name and image. Generally, there are four ways of promoting your business:

1. advertising,
2. public/media relations,
3. sales and
4. special promotional activities (i.e. trade shows, seminars, etc.)

Market Position

Your position is how you are perceived by your consumers. Successful positioning will allow you to develop an image, reinforce it, and secure a solid niche by building your business and developing loyal customers. Your image and position take time to develop, so you must continually reinforce it throughout the life of your business.

Often, your personal perceptions may differ from your consumers' and it is smart to survey them to learn how they feel about your business. If their perceptions differ from what you would like them to be, you need to develop repositioning strategies.

Developing a marketing position involves three basic steps.

1. *Assessing your current image and position.*

2. *Determining the market niche(s) you'd like to have.* What are the strengths and weaknesses in the current products/services offered by your competition? How can you fill these gaps?

3. *Developing appropriate strategies and provision of products/services to support your desired position.*

Push Marketing....

Producers may try to "push" a product through the channel of distribution by promoting it to the level or group closest to them. In service businesses, this is primarily done through referral sources. An accountant may approach business managers or consultants and encourage them to "push" referrals his/her way.

And Pull Marketing

A product can also be promoted using the "pull" strategy. This activity is directed at the end user in order to develop demand for the product. The idea is that consumers will demand the product from retailers, who in turn will demand it from wholesalers. This is what is referred to as a product being "pulled" through the channel. Advertising that targets the general public is the most prevalent "pull" marketing strategy.

The Business Life Cycle

There are four stages in this cycle: Introduction, Growth, Maturity and Decline. Your business may be in any one of these. Let's look at each in turn and find their basic characteristics. As you move through the stages, typically, you'll find that your marketing expenses will decrease.

The following is an example of how a printing business might move through the various phases.

The *Introduction* Stage is the phase in which the product/service is researched, planned, developed and introduced. The first promotional strategies are aimed at building name recognition, informing consumers of products/services offered and encouraging purchase.

> *Print Shop—When the shop opened, it was the only copy business in the neighborhood and was positioned as the "neighborhood copy shop." It provided the basics such as printing for both large and small quantities, featured pick up and delivery and provided basic typesetting capabilities. Ads were designed to inform people about its existence and its services.*

The *Growth* Phase of the product/service is the stage when there's an emphasis on improving distribution, customer satisfaction and developing strong referral sources. In this stage, consumers are very aware of the products/services you offer. Your marketing strategies are based on maintaining stability, quality and product/service improvement. Developing customer loyalty is imperative.

> *As the community grew, so did the printing business. Customers began to request a fax service, more sophisticated typesetting and graphic capabilities. Those services along with a desktop publishing system were added, and the shop even began selling office supplies. The print shop is no longer just a print shop for it offers many services at the request of its customers.*

The *Maturation* Phase is when the competition has declined (weaker rivals have failed), consumers are very aware of the services, although demand may start to slow down. Your marketing strategies should be based on maintaining stability, customer, loyalty and quality. Complacency can erode any business. Expenses, in general, are much lower than during the Introduction or Growth stages and revenues should be higher.

To keep customers loyal and add convenience, the management decided to let customers open accounts in which they're billed monthly. The business also set-up a discount program to high volume accounts, in addition to monthly promotions designed around the services and products offered.

The *Decline* Phase is when your product/service is perceived as no longer needed or the competition has become so aggressive that market share and revenues decline severely. Changing consumer behavior patterns contribute to a reduced demand. Marketing should be minimal, and the decision you face is whether to improve, alter, or terminate the product/service.

Over time, several new franchised print shops have opened in your area with major advertising support. They offer all the services you offer and a little more. Business has been lost to them due to their locations, services, etc. In order to compete with them, you must decide if you want to add the same services they offer, and/or increase your advertising budget to maintain your present niche.... Or should you accept the buy-out offer from this same franchise company and become one of their shops!

External Marketing

External marketing involves all the marketing efforts directed at bringing customers to your business. It includes the four major promotional tactics which are advertising, public/media relations, sales and special promotions. For additional information and marketing tools that fall within these groups, consult the following chapters.

Internal Marketing

Internal marketing activities refer to any marketing or communication activities directed toward groups inside or presently interacting with your business. For example, consult chapters on customer surveys, customer relations, in-store promotion and sales awards and incentives. It costs approximately five times more to get a new customer through external marketing than it does through maintaining loyal customers. So in terms of marketing costs, internal marketing is very important in helping to keep costs under control and in developing repeat business.

Market Research

Determining if you have a product/service that is really needed

Once you have conceptualized the service/product, you'll need a good marketing plan— and that often hinges on competent research. Major corporations spend millions of dollars to test new products. Typically, they will use geographic areas that are demographically representative of markets into which they want to expand. For example, a major tobacco company tested a new type of cigarette. Fitted with a plastic mouthpiece, the product was meant to reduce tar and nicotine consumption. After some months, they found these cigarettes were being used by crack cocaine smokers as an alternative to a pipe. The company quickly halted plans to produce the cigarette due to the potential for abuse. This research saved the company millions of dollars at a relatively early stage in the development process.

For the small business owner, there are several inexpensive testing methods. They include surveys, one-on-one interviews, and focus groups. Nearly any marketing decision can benefit from use of these tools. These testing tools are particularly crucial when:

1. a new product or service is being launched;

2. the decision maker is unclear on the background of the problem or of alternative solutions; and/or

3. the start-up costs are large.

Surveys are used with large population, or demographic samples. By definition, you seek to represent in your survey a specific target population, and you want your smaller sample to represent that target well. This type of quantitative research can provide important statistical information for your business. For example, how many people are aware your business exists, how many are interested in trying your product, what new product should you introduce next. All of these questions, which require numerical answers can best be answered by surveys. Surveys, however, are often far too expensive for the average small business owner. In that situation, you should detail for yourself the information you would want a survey to provide. With that list in hand, attempt to find other means to answer these very important questions. Maybe a small phone survey (not so statistically representative) done by some college students. Maybe a questionnaire handed out at a local meeting. With all of these alternatives, the problem will usually be that you won't have a representative sample. Your sample will undoubtedly end up biased in one way or another. Pay attention to that fact in making decisions based on these data. However, in almost all cases, some information will prove to be more insightful than no information.

One-on-one interviews are designed to get at more subjective and qualitative information. Should your box be blue or pink? What kinds of mental associations do consumers have with this name? Which logo is more professional looking? These types of qualitative judgments often use some form of interviewing techniques.

Focus groups are groups of representative consumers or potential buyers, usually 6-8 people, who are brought together for the purpose of discussing a specific topic. How do they pick golf clubs? What are they looking for in a doctor? The strength of different advertising campaigns. Again, the information being collected is largely qualitative, but this type of information can help you gain insight into your future marketing plans.

A full treatment of marketing research is beyond the scope of this book. You can find numerous books on this subject at your local library, and classes on this subject at your local college. Rather, our point here is that understanding your customers, their needs, wants and perceptions of your product or service is an important part of market planning and one in which you should be actively involved.

Reach & Frequency

A good marketing communication plan is based on two concepts —reach & frequency. The term reach refers to *the number of different people* who will be exposed to your messages in the media at least one time. If your business is new, reach may be a little more important than frequency because you'll want to develop awareness and get people to become familiar with your product/service. The wider the reach of the medium, the more expensive it will be to buy. Frequency refers to the number of times each person will be exposed to that message, and frequency becomes a little more important than reach once you've developed a defined audience with a basic level of awareness of your business. It can be difficult to achieve a balance because as reach increases, frequency decreases and visa versa. You need to have both at one time or another!

Every ad needs a minimum frequency before its message makes an impact. Studies indicate that the minimum is at least three times before it sinks in. So when planning your ad schedules be sure that you can reach the same audience at least three times or your money will be wasted. And because there are no guarantees, you will probably have to buy a minimum of six ads to be reasonable sure your audience hears or sees them. One of the best ways to achieve frequency is to be sure your ads runs in the same time slots or programs for electronic mediums and the same sections for print mediums. Since people generally listen to the radio or watch TV at the same times each day, you increase your chances for frequency. The same holds true for reading specific sections in a newspaper or magazine.

Target Marketing

Market Segmentation is the process of dividing a large market into smaller, similar subsets with the same needs and/or responsiveness to marketing offerings. That's like taking residents in a specific zip code zone (large market) and breaking it down into homeowners and renters (the subsets).

Demographic Segmentation is the information on age, sex, race, education, occupation, number in household, income and education that is critical in the consumer purchase process. Depending on the product/service, different demographic factors can have important impacts on buying behaviors. If you're selling luxury items, for example, it should be marketed only to those who can afford them and you will need to know the income, occupation and probably age of your targeted market.

Psychographics looks at variables such as lifestyle, consumer attitudes, interests and opinions. "Quality-minded" consumers look for the best product/service available, regardless of price. Others are ecologically conscious and may tend to seek out natural, environmentally-friendly products. Consumers can be feminists, have children, dislike unions, or prefer gourmet cooking— all of which may affect their buying behavior.

Behavioristic Segmentation, last but not least, segments consumers on the basis of their actual buying behavior. For example, a mail order catalog tracks exactly what is purchased, such as the name-brand of kitchen appliances or the type of children's toys. These businesses can then expand by offering customers with specific buying patterns, products that are likely to fit into that pattern.

After you have developed a list of all the segments and groups you can market to, it is important to prioritize them. Your primary targets should include only those segments that are the most cost effective and that can generate the highest return on your investment. Other target groups should be considered as back-up strategies. Don't spread yourself too thin; concentrate on only those groups which you think you can handle. If you've recently opened a video store in a family-oriented neighborhood, you'll want to stress the family videos you offer. Then once you've built your niche, you can begin to concentrate in another area.

Each of your target markets will need specific marketing approaches designed to reach each audience and generate a response. If you've done your research well, you should have lots of information which can be used to design a specific marketing program that will satisfy your target market(s) and get in them in your door.

Planning and Budgeting the Marketing Program

Marketing as an Investment

The money and time invested in your business must be viewed as an investment with long term payoffs; otherwise, you may be tempted not to expend your resources because results are not immediately forthcoming. The programs and practices you put into action to generate business must be laid out carefully with the intention that your business grows slowly and steadily over time.

With many small business people, money and time are two resources in short supply. Until now, your marketing strategies have probably been driven by the presence or absence of these two. Without planning, and intelligent commitment of resources, marketing becomes capricious, short term and ineffective.

A Marketing Mission

The most important activity you can perform in writing your marketing plan is to first develop organizational and marketing mission statements.

The organizational mission statement should address what business you are in, the purpose for it, and who you plan to serve. This may seem basic, but remember that services similar to yours have different priorities for conducting business. The following are mission statements. An organizational mission statement:

- To provide an excellent service/product in the community in which we serve.

- To offer a broad range of services/products to new markets.

- To grow and adapt to environmental changes in order to assure long-term survival.

A marketing mission statement includes:

- The purpose for marketing your business.

- Why you're developing a marketing plan.

- The target markets you'll pursue through your efforts.

The following is an example of a marketing mission statement for an interior designer:

1. Develop a mutually beneficial relationship with furniture outlets.

2. Increase cash flow.

3. Expand the range of services and modify existing services to increase referrals.

4. Change my image to be more on-line with the furniture outlets' clientele.

5. Develop a strategic plan for growth of the services to include all of the stores' locations.

Mission statements should be modified and updated as the marketplace changes. Be sure to keep your statements brief and to the point. Mission statements will provide the groundwork for developing your specific marketing goals and objectives.

Planning Your Budget

There is an old adage that says you must plan your work and then work your plan. Planning is the key to marketing, and should be based on the research you have conducted previously as well as internal and external analyses.

Internal analysis includes examining your product/service and identifying its strengths and weaknesses. The external analysis shows what's happening in your business in general and the activities of your competition.

Be sure your marketing plan complements your business plan. For instance, if your business plan is projecting an annual 25% increase in sales, your marketing plan should be specifically designed to increase sales volume.

Implementation

This is the most difficult phase for most self-marketers. A well-conceived plan will end up sitting on a shelf unless it is put into action. Because of your limited resources, you must know before-hand and be committed to the allocation of a specific amount of time and money.

A rule of thumb for projecting a budget: allocate approximately 10% of your forecasted gross revenues if you're just starting out or introducing a new product/service. Plan on using approximately five percent for mature businesses and two percent for declining businesses.

Your time allocation is as important as your budget. First, think about how much your time is worth. If you are receiving an average of $50 per hour for your services, this is your time cost. Any other activities you pursue should return at least this much on your time investment. Often it is better to use someone less expensive per hour to accomplish some of your marketing activities, but you will need to devote a certain amount of time per week yourself to your marketing program. Time is money— use your time as efficiently as possible.

Setting Goals and Objectives

Marketing goals and objectives represent the results you wish to achieve, and establish the direction you will take with all of your marketing efforts.

Marketing goals are meant to outline the results and the outcomes you want to attain, as well as to establish the basis for developing objectives. They might involve creating a new business, increasing profitability or staff size, or increasing your referral sources.

A simple, yet common goal: *"Increase my sales by 20%"*

Marketing objectives are the specific and measurable results which you hope to accomplish. Measurement can include time frames, number of customers and levels of revenue. Although it is important to define goals and objectives, you need to be realistic and understand that you are really trying to predict future results.

Your goals and objectives are not set in concrete; they provide a flexible direction for you to take in the design and implementation of your plan.

Examine the following objective—it is a POOR example of an objective, as it does not give us measurable facts on which to base an evaluation: "Increase the number of new clients who register in the community."

A better, more measurable objective would be: *"Increase by 15% the number of new clients who register in my service area by Sept. 1, 199_."*

This objective has told us who (new clients in the service area) did what (registered), by how much (15%) and by when (Sept. 1, 199_). It is specific, quantifiable and measurable, and can be used to accurately gauge the effectiveness of the plan.

Setting Your Goals

Goal setting is the first step in a marketing program. Having a clear picture of short and long term goals is important in deciding which marketing tactics to use.

Goals reflect your expectation. They are the results you want to produce for yourself and for your business. They might involve creating new business, increasing profitability, increasing your staff, purchasing a new home or providing for your retirement. Because you need to be able to measure your progress, be sure to state your goals in a tangible way.

Some marketing advisors advocate making the goals pertain to your business only. We do not agree; your individual goals and objectives will have significant bearing on your business. We advise you to record both personal and business goals, preferably as two separate sets. Or, have at least one personal goal for every three business goals you make.

A good way to approach goal setting is to work backward. Start somewhere in the future, say five or ten years, and list three to five results you want to have produced by then. Then work backward to the present—for example, three years, one year, six months and three months.

As you move back, the goal statements should get more and more detailed so that the three-month goals are very specific. With written goals, you know where you are heading and you can identify the things that will and will not help you get there. Update your goals on a quarterly basis so that you always have a set to work on.

One more word about goals: they should be at least 50 percent doable. That is, a goal gives you something to strive for, rather than representing what you know you can accomplish. For example, if you know that you can bring in a net income of $4,000 over the next three months, set a goal at $6,000 or $8,000 and then go for it! You'll be amazed at the results you can produce.

The following is an example of one individual's goals.

Ten-Year Goals

I will retire from my business and turn it over to my junior partner. I will have sufficient financial security to allow me to choose my activities based on interest rather than on need. I will be firmly established as a speaker in my field, with at least three speaking engagements per year.

Five-Year Goals

I will have a junior partner in the business. I will have a contract with a publisher for a book in my field with at least a $5,000 advance payment. I will have at least one week's vacation per quarter.

Three-Year Goals

I will own a new home. I will have a minimum net income of $50,000 per year. I will be publishing at least two articles per year at $500 per article.

One-Year Goals

I will set up my retirement plan. I will take a minimum three week vacation to Europe. I will add three new clients per month.

Six-Month Goals

I will add two new clients per month. I will join a new networking group and generate at least three referrals per month. I will have at least two three-day weekends as vacation time.

Three-Month Goals

I will have a minimum net income of $6,000, approximately $2,000 per month. I will add one new client per month. I will paint my living room and redecorate my bedroom.

Strategies to Achieve Your Goals

Strategies outline the plan of action, in order to accomplish your objectives. Strategies give focus to your marketing efforts and allow you to clearly describe how you will approach your target groups.

Strategies are determined by the stage of the marketing life cycle your business is in. Regardless of your product/service, there are five general strategies which you can use to accomplish your objectives.

Market Penetration involves attracting more business to your current services in your marketplace or taking business away from your competitors.

Market Expansion involves attracting more business to your current services in an expanded market by increasing your service area.

Vertical Integration involves adding to what you already offer by merging or associating with a business similar to yours or through the use of cooperatives or takeovers.

Horizontal Integration involves attracting new business by adding new services not previously offered.

Diversification involves adding new services usually considered outside of your line of business.

Marketing Tactics

Tactics, also called activities, specify the exact steps needed to implement each strategy. The following is an example of one "branch" of a marketing "tree." It begins with a mission statement and ends with related tactics:

Mission: "Increase cash flow and revenue."
Goal #1:   "Increase referrals to by business"
Objective #1: "Increase referrals by 25% in the next quarter"
Strategy #1:   "Promote my services to potential new referral
               sources"

Tactic #1:	"Join local chamber of commerce"
Tactic #2:	"Join networking group in my area"
Tactic #3:	"Advertise in appropriate referral source journals, newsletters, etc."

Evaluation and Modification

Because every marketing plan has objectives that are specific, measurable and quantifiable, you can concretely evaluate the performance of the plan. Assume, for instance, that your goal is to "increase revenues by 25% over the next year." But you find at the end of the quarter your revenues are only up 15%—you have obviously not met your stated objective.

Marketing plans are 40 percent scientific and 60 percent creative. They are flexible and can be changed to suit the changing needs and wants of your market groups. But if you don't have criteria with which to track and measure results, you will never know what is working and what is not.

By evaluating your plan, you can modify either your tactics, to bring them in line with your stated objectives, or your objectives, to make them more realistic.

A Word About Marketing Professionals

Hiring a marketing professional to help can be daunting. What if, after paying hundreds or thousands of dollars nothing happens? A valid question, but it applies to your own efforts as well. It is sadly not uncommon that a business owner, after many months and dollars of self-implemented market efforts, looks back and realizes that the results-to-expense ratio is too low.

A marketing specialist can be an excellent boost to your business. She/he can help you avoid expensive dead-end strategies while getting the most out of the marketing plans you do implement. She/he will devise strategies specifically for your business and will provide the required expertise. While using a consultant does not preclude your having some marketing how-how, you can take advantage of his or her experience in that industry. Costs can be quite reasonable, especially if you keep in mind that the expense in an *investment*, to be measured by the long-range results that occur.

For guidelines on evaluating and hiring a professional, consult the chapter on Advertising.

Marketing Action Plan for June 1, 199___ Aug. 31, 199___

1. GOAL: Increase referrals to my business

1. Strategy: Promote my services to potential new referral sources

1. Objective: Increase referrals by 25% over first quarter

Specific Targeted Markets	Tactic	Time Frame	Cost	Expected Results
1. Business managers/consultants	1A Join chamber of Commerce and attend functions	June 1	$200.00	3 new referrals by Aug. 31
	1B Join a business "networking" group and attend weekly meetings	July 16	$150.00	3 new referrals by Aug. 31
	1C Advertise in print media as needed	1 ad/month in 3 print guides	$1,000.00	4 new referrals by Aug. 31
	1D Direct mail to managers/consultants in the county	Aug. 1	$1,500.00	5 new referrals by Aug. 31
	1E Sales calls to recipients of direct mail	Aug. 5-15	Time	5 new referrals by Aug. 31

Self-Assessment Tools

Set #1: Your Marketing Personality

These questions help you evaluate your comfort level with marketing as it applies to your business. Give yourself 5 points for each statement you answer with a yes.

1. I realize it takes time/money to market my business and I am comfortable with this.

2. I currently have a brochure that is bringing in business.

3. I know how my customers first hear about me.

4. I know my marketing strengths and weaknesses.

5. I know what the features/benefits are of my business.

6. I have lots of ideas about how to market my business.

7. I currently have a Yellow Pages ad that is bringing in business.

8. I use my memberships in peer groups and/or business organizations to promote my business.

9. I have contacts in related business fields who refer customers to me.

A score of 35–45 means you are comfortable and knowledgeable about marketing your business. You may need to spend time evaluating what is effective and focusing your efforts on those specific activities.

A score of 24–34, means you have a moderate comfort level and knowledge of how to market your business. You are in a position to experiment with different tactics before deciding on what is right for you.

A score of 16–24 means you are uncomfortable with marketing your business and lack the experience to do so. First, consider using a basic referral development strategy, that is to approach family, friends in your social circle and professionals who know you to begin marketing your business. See what their needs are and, if appropriate, offer your services. Pretty soon you will gain confidence.

A score of below 15, means you need to learn more about each of the different marketing tactics and assess your comfort level before pursuing them.

Set #2: Your Business Personality

These questions apply to your current business practices. Give yourself 5 points for each statement you answer with a yes.

1. I know exactly what products/services I am offering.
2. I know clearly who my potential customers are.
3. I have a name and graphic image for my business.
4. My business location is easily accessible.
5. My business location is attractive and comfortable.
6. The telephone access to my business works well for current and prospective customers.
7. My hours are convenient for my customers.

A score of 25-35 means you have a strong sense of what your business is about, what your customers need and the importance of maintaining satisfied customers and referral sources.

A score of 15-24 means you need to develop your position (image) and offer products/services consistent with that image and with what your customers want.

A score of less than 15, means you must first address your present and desired position by surveying your users about how they perceive you and their overall satisfaction with your business.

Set #3: Your Personality

This last set is focused on your personal traits and talents. Whenever possible it's wise to implement marketing strategies that will take advantage of your personal strengths. Give yourself 5 points for each statement you answer with a yes.

1. I'm a creative thinker.
2. I have no problem introducing myself to strangers at business or social functions.
3. I am outgoing and interested in others.
4. I enjoy conversing with my peers.
5. I enjoy initiating contact with potential customers.
6. I enjoy public speaking.
7. I enjoy presenting at seminars and workshops.
8. I'm a talented writer.
9. I enjoy participating in networking groups.
10. I'm an organized person.

A score of over 35. You appear very comfortable with yourself and what you do. You are able to share both of these aspects with people in a direct way.

A score of 25–34. You are comfortable with yourself as a business person but not necessarily as a marketer. You probably need to develop your marketing confidence by using "softer" approaches such as one-to-one referral development.

A score below 15. You might consider getting some coaching and/ or support of your marketing efforts through networking, public speaking courses or concentrating more on introverted tactics such as writing letters of introduction, articles, press releases and newsletters.

Explanation of Symbols

Each marketing tool in the handbook is accompanied by a set of symbols. These provide a "quick glance" reference of the resources needed to implement the various marketing strategies. In many cases, you will see more than one symbol. For example, you will see a $$ and a symbol for time—that means the cost of implementing the tool will have a moderate cost and a minimal time commitment.

Financial Commitment

Every marketing task takes money, some more than others. This symbol indicates the magnitude of financial commitment necessary to implement the task successfully.

$ = low cost, $$ = moderate,

$$$ = high, $$$$ = expensive

Time

Time is another ever present and limited resource. The amount of time needed to implement for different marketing tactics may vary dramatically.

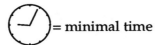 = minimal time

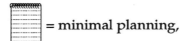 = moderate amount of time

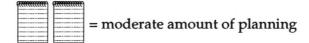 = time intensive

Planning

The notepad is for tasks that require a high degree of planning for implementation.

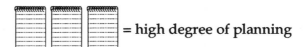 = minimal planning,

= moderate amount of planning

= high degree of planning

Consulting

 This symbol notes areas where outside services are or may be advisable. The type of service may vary, although all can be provided through a marketing consultant.

In addition to the symbols for money, time and planning, you'll also see a symbol for the marketing category that the tool/tactic falls within.

Advertising

 This symbol indicates the tool is an advertising function and will in nearly all cases cost money to use.

Public Relations

 This indicates a public relations function and often requires more of a time commitment that a financial commitment.

Sales Promotion

 This lets you know it's a sales promotion tool.

Customer Relations

 This means it's a customer relations function and an internal marketing tool.

The Marketing Tools

Advertising... a Definition

A textbook definition of advertising is "the non-personal communication of information, usually paid for and usually persuasive in nature, about product ideas, or services by the identified sponsors through various media" (Bovee, *Contemporary Advertising*).

Advertising as we know it usually refers to mass media advertising through electronic (television, radio, cable) and print (magazines, newspapers, etc.) mediums. These types of communication channels provide the broadest visibility and the ability to specifically target your markets.

Traditionally, advertising has been an expensive marketing strategy. But in recent years, the cost of using mass media has become more affordable because of the competition between network and cable TV stations, and the number of new radio stations, community newspapers and specialty magazines. But even with the competition, it can still be costly to produce and run a mass media ad campaign.

Prior to any advertising, you should consider your objectives. Not all businesses, especially small business will benefit or need to appeal to a mass market. Many businesses have a very specific and narrow niche of people to serve.

Image advertising, the most expensive, is done to create or enhance the image you want to promote - it's not necessarily done to make an immediate sale. Whereas direct advertising is targeted to referral sources and/or individuals who have the most potential for an immediate need to use your products/services.

For small businesses advise using a variety of direct marketing tactics. Selective advertising combined with other marketing tactics can be a powerful tool. But prior to making any advertising decision, you need to know whether the medium reaches your target audience. You can obtain this information by asking the ad reps for a media kit, which includes all the information an advertiser needs to know about the medium.

TV, especially the national networks, is typically the least targeted and most expensive way of advertising. Radio will give you a more targeted audience and it's less expensive. The print media offer even more targeting potential and generally is less expensive than the electronic media. Lastly, direct mail allows you to target any type of consumer you may choose. A direct mail piece has a "call to action," such as a response card, coupon or an 800 number that the recipient can use. Mailing lists can be purchased that incorporate geographic, demographic and psychographic variables. Unfortunately, the more specific your list, the more money you will pay, and response rates from direct mail are typically very low at about 2%.

If you're planning a very large advertising campaign, more than four different mediums such a TV, newspapers, magazines or billboards, it would be to your advantage to consult an advertising specialist to produce and place effective ads. Also remember that once an ad is produced, it can be used repeatedly with little or no change.

The following are helpful hints you can use when evaluating and selecting an advertising agency. The right agency will:

1. Specialize in your area.

2. Make you feel comfortable and work as part of your team.

3. Be effective at its own marketing.

4. Be relationship-oriented.

5. At the first meeting have you do 95% of the talking.

6. Make it clear that you know your business, and they know marketing.

7. Articulate a marketing philosophy that makes sense to you.

8. Present a commitment and capability for implementing a proper marketing mix.

9. Won't try to break your budget.

Be leery of agencies that:

1. Insists your company's image needs to be changed.

2. Criticize your current advertising.

3. Recommend you produce an expensive company brochure.

4. Tell you "Here's what you should be spending on advertising."

5. Can't provide client references.

6. Seem to believe they know more about your business than you do.

Advertising Specialties

see: gift certificates

Advertising specialties are items on which the advertiser imprints a message to remind a potential customer of your services/products. These types of items are designed to increase awareness by keeping your name in front of your targeted market. They come in the form of pens, pencils, notepads, refrigerator magnets, T-shirts, visors and much more. Such items have a long life and provide on-going visibility. Specialty items are not meant to serve as a primary marketing medium, but rather as a supplemental promotional effort.

Be sure that your specialty item relates to your business. For example, it makes sense for an auto repair business to give-away key chains or a stationery store to use notepads. When writing your copy, keep the item in mind. Not much will fit on a pen, whereas you can say more on a calendar. Remember to keep it from looking too much like an ad and select an item that is appropriate for your market.

Companies specializing in these items are found in the yellow pages under "advertising specialties." Call to set up a meeting with a sales representative or have them send you a catalog. Explore the catalog for items that fit your business and don't be afraid to ask the sales rep for any suggestions. It's a good idea to consult with more than one company as merchandise and prices vary.

Specialty items are meant to be ordered in volume which can be expensive. For example a pen with your business name and logo may cost $.75 each, but often there is a minimum order of 500.

Business Gifts

A business gift is a good public relations tool...after all everyone enjoys getting a present. Gifts can be given for a variety of reasons—to develop new business, say thanks to loyal referrals and customers, to motivate employees and to keep your name visible. A business gift is a little different from specialty items, in that it is sent, given or delivered to someone specific and accompanied with a personal card or note.

The most obvious time of year is the Christmas holiday, but often the most appreciated gifts are those that are least expected such as a birthday, anniversary, promotion or some other special occasion.

In general, business customers should receive gifts that are of use at the office, while consumer customers should receive something appropriate for the home. This form of targeted marketing will provide you visibility in each market where it will do the most good.

In most cases of gift giving—it's the thought that counts, and not necessarily the cost or the size of the gift. But different situations call for different gifts.

Advertorials

see: articles for publication, display ads, media relations

Advertorials can serve as a highly effective marketing tool. Just as the term implies, advertorials can be defined as part advertisement, part editorial. Essentially, they are paid for articles which usually appear in magazines to create awareness and generate sales for a business. This style of advertising works well for professionals because it provides the opportunity to describe a service in detail whether it deals with a new medical procedure, a time-saving device or a service for home improvement. Generally, you as the advertiser write your own article, but in some cases, the publication may have a staff member write it for you as part of the ad's cost. Since an advertorial is paid for, you have final copy approval before it's printed—and this where the advertorial differs from the standard newspaper article that appears in an editorial section. If the story is written by a reporter, at no cost to you then you do not have control over the article's content. Sometimes a photo or illustration can be included in the advertorial.

Advertorials are often difficult to distinguish from news features and other editorial. Much of the appeal comes from the fact that they look like news and people are far more likely to read them. Businesses often place ads next to advertorials to create a "double whammy" effect.

Unlike the typical advertisement, the advertorial allows the business person to tell the story about the business, giving the reader a more complete picture.

Advertorials have become a big business—you'll find magazines such as *Time* and *Business Week* regularly feature special advertorial sections on subjects ranging from health to duty-free goods.

If you write your own advertorial, the following are some suggestions and guidelines.

- Study the publication you intend to use so that your copy is as close to the publication's style as possible. Advertorials are supposed to look like a news story whether it's a serious article or one that is more feature-oriented.

New Concept for Printing in The '90's

There has been a radical change in the printing industry since the early '80. Computers have infiltrated the industry. Accounting and quoting software have been developed to help even the smallest print shops. However, the most remarkable change has transformed the world of topography. Traditional typesetting has entered the computer age. With the use of computers, print shops can now create exciting text and beautiful graphic pictures at a minimal cost, compared with the traditional method of having to use a graphic artist, typesetter, paste-up artist and expensive duplication machines.

Print shops are literally becoming small Ad-Agencies. Using desk top computers to create entire publications and presentations. Servati Graphics is a neighborhood print shop that uses this new medium to its fullest. They specialize in computer graphics and use the computer to show TYPE in a whole new light. They are a commercial printing and advertising service specializing in concept-to-completion. Additionally they offer custom multicolor printing, design and typesetting. Servati Graphics is the Print Shop of the '90's.

We feature Crane and other quality papers.
619.456.2882

7520 EADS AVENUE • LA JOLLA, CALIFORNIA

- You want it to appear credible and believable. In some respects, an advertorial is similar to a press release, but is more sales oriented. Since you are paying for the space, you can include all of the details you feel are important in selling your product or service.

- Include strong facts about the product, for example: why it's unique or great, how it differs, how it was developed and by whom if appropriate.

- Create a catchy title.

- Write a good lead paragraph to grab and hold the reader's attention.

- Include some quotes by an appropriate endorser, by someone who has used the product, or both.

- Be sure to include where to find the product/service—your address, phone number and logo.

Articles for Publication

see: advertorials, newsletters

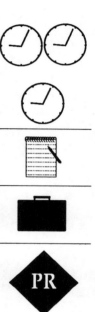

If you have a flair for writing, along with the time and effort to commit, then writing for publications can be a great marketing tool. You can write feature articles for magazines or journals, send letters to the editor, or author a book in your area of expertise. Any of these avenues can be used to communicate important information about your business. And once published, information can be widely shared and repeatedly used.

Writing articles for publication works well for professionals and service-oriented businesses. For example, if you are a chef and you teach gourmet cooking classes, you may want to create a complete holiday brunch for the food section of your local newspaper using your original recipes or your patrons' favorite recipes. If you are an image consultant, write a lifestyle feature detailing how to dress 10 pounds thinner through the use of accessories. But before you go to the effort of writing anything consult with the editor. She may not be interested in your specific idea, but perhaps can offer different story angle.

Writing for any kind of publication can earn you respect, enhance your credentials, provide visibility and build your reputation. But keep in mind, when you are writing as the expert, you must present an unbiased article. As the author of an article, you are perceived as the expert and therefore people will seek your services. This type of public relations is not for promoting your business directly. To write about only your business would be considered an advertorial and would usually be channeled through the advertising department.

In addition to newspapers and magazines, professional organizations often publish national journals or even a local chapter newsletters. These publications are also a good avenue because they are very targeted and writing for them can familiarize your peers with your business. In most cases, you have more leeway in writing about your specific business. Your contribution will enhance your status among fellow professionals, and may well also increase referrals by peers.

The Query Letter

To get your story idea considered, especially for magazines and newspapers, you will need a query letter. This is a letter that inquires about an editor's interest in a specific idea whether it deals with a subject, a trend or an event. This letter can be used to get yourself a by-line (if you propose writing the story yourself), or to be included in a news/feature story that positions you as an expert or mentions your business in the context of the article.

A query letter should be brief, but should clearly state your story idea, the angle from which you would approach it, why it would be of interest to the publication's readers, the length of the article and a publication date. And if you are offering to write the story, include a brief bio highlighting your expertise and your writing experience. If you have had published articles be sure to list them.

The only real cost to you is your time and brain power. The reprints can be used in your press kit to promote your business whether it's product or service-oriented. Be aware that proper writing procedure and style are essential to being published.

Billboards

see: display ads, placards

Billboards are everywhere you look and are another avenue to create visibility for your business. They are a very specialized medium that tends to work for businesses such as recreational facilities and attractions, hotels, motels, restaurants or a unique shopping complex that is off the main road.

Billboards are used to create visibility and not necessarily to sell a product. They work best if your goal is to create an image for your business by establishing a logo or colors. But for billboards to be effective, they must be well placed and cleverly designed. Wording needs to be simply stated and if it is used to direct customers to your hard-to-find location, directions must be very clear.

Another advantage this medium offers is that it can be cost effective for reaching thousands of people with one ad. In most cases, the same people see the same sign regularly, for example, on their way to work. Billboards are also flexible and can be changed seasonally. But even with all the advantages, billboards are often still considered an expensive way for a small business to advertise.

The medium is not a wise choice for reaching very specific or narrow markets, with the exception of commuters. Some people find them offensive, especially those that are environmentally-conscious because they believe they clutter the landscape.

One last word, while in some cases billboards can be cost effective, they are not cheap. They often must be purchased in 3, 6 or 12 month contracts and of course, the best locations will be the most expensive!

Brochures

see: direct mail, flyers, image, packaging

A brochure is a promotional piece developed to sell your business, whether it is a product or service. The simplest brochures are letter-size sheets folded into a two or three-panel piece. Others resemble booklets, with pages that turn rather than fold. There are many ways to format and design a brochure, but the content is the most important part of your brochure and its purpose is to inform the reader with the intention of selling.

Brochures are a valuable marketing tool in cases where more than one service is offered or the product has many uses. For example, let's use a gift basket business. In addition to the 10 standard packages to cover such occasions as weddings, baby showers and birthdays, which the brochure describes in detail, you can also describe how you design custom baskets and list as many themes you can come up with. Also included would be delivery information, leadtime, hours of business, etc.

If you have a professional service, you would include your qualifications, background, specialty, and when appropriate, affiliations, philosophies, qualified staff and accepted insurance plans.

This marketing tool must be factual, yet interesting and easy to read. The type face you choose should also be easy to look at and read. It should be designed to let potential clients know about all the services you offer and why you are better than the competition.

A brochure can be designed to be hand-delivered, available to peers to be displayed in their offices, included in a media kit or mailed as a direct mail piece. It's a tangible item and provides credibility in the eyes of customers and clients. Brochures have a great deal of potential and they should not be produced in a rush. Brainstorm with a professional and get assistance with the design, copy and production of the piece.

Don't be afraid to use artwork and photos to keep it visually interesting and to further explain and sell!

Bulletin Boards

see: classified ads, display ads, flyers/inserts, door hangers

Bulletin boards can be a very inexpensive way to create visibility for your business and work well for those on a tight budget or no budget at all. Bulletin boards are one place to begin, especially if you have a part-time or seasonal business. They can be found in a variety of places, from churches, to retail and specialty stores, to laundry mats and even professional offices. All you need is a professional looking flyer/sign, highlighting what you do and how you can be contacted. If you offer free estimates or samples, be sure to include that. Take the time to present a flyer that is clearly written and looks professional. You may even want to have it typeset, and include a graphic or two so that it's visually interesting.

Business Cards/Stationery/ Collateral Materials

see: Identity/Image of your business

Business cards, stationery, envelopes and other tools used in your business are referred to as *collateral materials*. Collateral materials also include a logo if you have one, presentation folders, rolodex cards, brochures and administration forms used in billing, etc. Like it or not, these items combined will create part of your company's image.

The logo is a symbol used to identify a business and can give the business a personality. If your business name doesn't clearly say what you do, then you should probably include a simple line that makes it clear the type of business you provide such as JONES & ASSOCIATES...Commercial Real Estate Appraisers. Every business should have some kind of logo, and it should be included on all your materials and in your advertising. It can be as simple as the way your name is printed or it can be a separate, elaborate graphic or picture.

A logo is very important. It sets you apart from other companies in the same business, and it sets the tone of a business' image. Care should be taken when having one designed because the wrong image can give the wrong impression of your business, creating a negative effect. Also be sure the logo is one you expect to see in your industry. The style of your logo should generally be in keeping with the type of business you have. For example, clown logos would probably not work for the office of the attorney.

Designing business cards and stationery can be done by a graphic artist, or you can do it yourself with the help of your print shop. Most print shops have books with many different type styles and design layouts for you to choose from. If you already know what you want, take a sketch to your printer and have them typeset it and get it camera ready. Make sure your business cards, stationery, rolodex cards and other collateral materials are consistent in color, paper stock when appropriate, type face, design layout, etc. When your collateral materials are consistent, you present a more professional appearance which is particularly important to a new business. Over time people will come to recognize and associate your logo and materials with your company and its growing reputation.

md Communications

marketing communications
public relations

555 1st Avenue
San Diego, CA 92037

mary doe
(619) 555-1111
Fax: 555-1112

STANDARD BUSINESS CARD 2" x 3 1/4

---

md Communications
marketing communications/public relations
555 1st Avenue
San Diego, CA 92037

#10 ENVELOPE

---

md Communications
marketing communications / public relations

(619) 555-1111 • Fax: 555-1112 • 555 1st Avenue • San Diego, CA 92037

STANDARD LETTERHEAD - 8 1/2" x 11"

---

md Communications

marketing communications / public relations
(619) 555-1111 • Fax: 555-1112

special events • promotions
media relations

555 1st Avenue • San Diego, CA 92037

ROLODEX CARD

This is a basic inexpensively designed package for a communications consultant. There isn't really a logo, but the design is consistent throughout the collateral materials. The graphics are very simple. Since, her business is communication, she has several choices when it comes to color. A standard blue ink would work well, or she could even use a red or purple ink.

LAW OFFICES OF
SMITH, DUNN & GRAY

JOHN SMITH
ATTORNEY AT LAW

111 4TH STREET, SUITE 200
SAN DIEGO, CA 99999

(619) 555-1111
Fax: 555-1112

STANDARD BUSINESS CARD 2" x 3 1/4

LAW OFFICES OF
SMITH, DUNN & GRAY
111 4TH STREET, SUITE 200
SAN DIEGO, CA 99999
(619) 555-1111
Fax 555-1112

LAW OFFICES OF
SMITH, DUNN & GRAY
111 4TH STREET, SUITE 200
SAN DIEGO, CA 99999

#10 ENVELOPE

STANDARD LETTERHEAD - 8 1/2" x 11"

An attorney must often be more traditional, using upper and low case, more serious type face and conservative colors such as black or gray.

When choosing type, pick type faces that are easy to read and that will work for all your needs such as stationery, business cards and advertising. There are type faces that look very serious, or very casual and some that even look whimsical. Be sure that what you select matches your business. Type faces that are appropriate for attorneys and accountants, don't necessarily work for designers and retail stores. Don't be afraid to see what other businesses in your industry are doing.

Cable Television

see: television

Most of what is true in creating a message for TV is true with the cable channels, but with cable you have more flexibility. You can get longer commercial times, and those advertisements can be more targeted to specific groups because of cable's narrower fields of interest. There are channels just for sports, comedy, health and movies.

Infomercials

Cable also offers a unique format called the "infomercial" which is similar to the advertorials found in the printed mediums. Infomercials are long ads. While they are used to sell the product/ service, they also provide helpful hints and detailed information about how that product/service is used, its advantages and usually a product demonstration. They don't look like traditional ads. Only after you've watched an infomercial for a few minutes will you realize that it is not a regular program.

Infomercials work for almost all types of businesses from automobile and fitness products, to plastic surgeons and home improvement items. But the one requisite for the product is that it be visual or that its product benefits be easily visualized or verbalized on camera. You must also have a spokesperson(s) who is very relaxed and confident.

The biggest obstacle in creating an infomercial will be the production cost in producing the ad. It can be very expensive. However, once it is produced, it can be used repeatedly in a variety of ways including at trade shows or in in-store promotions.

Catalogs

see: direct advertising response, mail order

A catalog order business often begins with a few original products or a single line of products. Your best bets are for those that are consumable, then you are assured of repeat business. Otherwise you'll be constantly on the prowl for new items.

Catalogs are another form of mail order, and knowing how to evaluate a product/service to find a niche is a key to being successful once you've got a catalog of items. One of the most important elements is to know who you're trying to sell to. Do your research to get a good profile of your typical customer or the customer you want to reach. Make sure you have good mailing lists—they are your only means of talking to your market, so know how your lists are developed.

When selecting merchandise for a catalog business, choose items that photograph well or that can be illustrated! Seeing the product is your best pitch. Try to keep a central theme because that's proven to be the most successful. By themes we mean, a catalog that features kitchen gadgets, personalized products, home services, apparel or convenience.

In searching for new sellables to expand your business or to replace outdated items, your best bet is to read, and read a lot...general consumer and trade magazines, newspapers and other catalogs. Attend trade shows, talk to manufacturers, visit boutiques, browse fairs and even foreign shops and publications. Once you've seen a specific item featured several times, then consider including it in your catalog if it's appropriate. For a catalog to be successful, it must be viewed as being worth looking at and acting upon. This means consumers should view your catalog as being unique, with items that are not easily available somewhere else. You would like your catalog to be a value to be received, with the authority to sell what it offers, and with a customer base that is satisfied with the products and service. (The latter usual means including a guaranteed satisfaction clause.)

Another way to use catalogs is to get your product into an already existing catalog that offers merchandise similar to yours. By going this route, you do not incur production or mailing costs. Each catalog operates differently, so once you've discovered one that is appropriate for you, do some research to find out whom to contact, then send a letter and perhaps a sample of your product.

Classified Advertising

see: display advertising, advertorial

Most people think classified ads are used exclusively for finding a job or selling a car, but classified ads can also successfully support a business service, product or professional practice.

There are three main places you can run a classified ad: magazines, daily newspapers and classified-ad newspapers. Also worth considering are trade publications, and association and club newsletters.

Classified ads are low priced, with discounts given for increased frequency. The cost of an ad is based on the number of lines, the number of words or the number of column inches, depending on the publication.

For businesses that are service-oriented, consider coming up with some sort of product to include in your ad. Produce a booklet, brochure, audiotape, or a videocassette that informs the reader about some issue in your area of expertise and advertise it as a free giveaway, or offer it for sale at a reasonable price. The expense is worth it because you will be adding names to your mailing lists for other marketing uses (see Databases).

Here are some suggestions in writing a good classified ad:

1. Use a headline that grabs attention. Be sure to keep it short.

2. Don't use abbreviations unless you are sure the reader will understand them.

3. Write in short, factual sentences. Try not to sound like a want ad.

4. Create a curiosity to find out more about your service or the desire to buy your product by being clear and simple. Omit certain facts such as cost or location. You want to generate a response so that you can follow through personally.

5. Always include a way to contact you—phone number or address.

6. Choose the section carefully, and consider placing your ad in more than one category. Make your ad stand out from other ads in the same section.

7. Be aware that writing a good classified ad is not easy, consult a pro if you really want to be successful.

Below is an example of how a classified ad can be used to support a service...in this case, for an interior designer specializing in the interior design of dental offices. This might appear in a local dental society newsletter.

MAKE YOUR OFFICE'S INTERIOR DESIGN AN INVESTMENT...

And get 100% return on your money. Interior design consultant with a specialty in designing dental offices. Ability to create a total office environment to reflect your personal tastes, increase staff's job satisfaction and cater to patients' needs. Call for a free brochure. Mary Doe, phone number, or an address to write for the brochure.

Below is another example of a classified ad that might appear in newspapers' classified ad sections or if you're targeting women, could be placed in publications specifically designed to reach women.

GET A PAYCHECK WHENEVER YOU WANT ONE...

be your own boss and never leave your home. Call for information on our home assembly programs—you can earn hundreds of dollars weekly. No experience necessary, call this phone number today.

Community Involvement/Charities

**see: peer group marketing, networking
through associations**

In recent years, the public at large has become conscious of what and how businesses give back to their communities. Involvement of this nature is a strong public relations tool that can build a positive image for a business owner(s) and garner increased visibility for your business. Showing an interest and supporting a good cause can be done in the form of donated time, money or materials. This is also another way to introduce your business into new markets. But remember the first objective is to gain business and secondly, know when to say NO! When selecting an organization to become involved with, you should consider the following:

- Does it make sense for me or my business?

  If your business or professional service is related to children, it makes sense choose an organization that involves children.

- Does this organization have the right image?

  Each group has a personality with specific demographics. If your business is geared to a young professional crowd, make sure you find a group with those demographics, either by asking the charity's director or attend some function on your own, before making a commitment.

- Can they benefit from what you have to offer? If you offer a specific service, can they benefit from you, and you from them.

- Do you want to support a large or small charity group or a community/civic cause?

  This is more of a personal choice, but do consider how it relates to your business.

Conferences

see: seminars, networking, public speaking, workshops

A conference is an obvious opportunity for networking with peers and potential clients. If you are an effective public speaker, being a presenter at a conference is also an excellent way to market yourself and your business. When you speak to a group of professionals, think of them as potential business. Your presentation must relate to the theme of the event, but it should also be related to your business.

Conferences are time intensive if you are a guest speaker.

Whether you're a speaker or an attendee, conferences provide the opportunity to meet a large number of people in a concentrated amount of time. The risk and expense of promoting the event are the sponsor's responsibility. Additionally, you can often rent an exhibit booth or set up a display which allows for direct contact with large numbers of people and greater visibility. Sometimes the conference sponsors will give you a booth in addition to or in exchange for your speaking.

Conference literature usually gives promotional information about each presenter, which is another good way to receive recognition and visibility—even among people not attending. Besides paying for exhibit space, the only real cost is your time. Unfortunately, the quality and success of the conference is not in your control.

Contests

see: cross-marketing, sales promotion

A contest is one of many promotional activities conducted on behalf of businesses looking to generate exposure and gain visibility. The definition of a contest is when skill is used in the game such as a drawing or costume contest, while the definition of a sweepstakes is a game of chance. With either, the advantages are that when done properly, they require a lot of consumer participation, add excitement to the advertising theme and/or interest in the product. But be careful—in some areas contests are prohibited.

Contests and sweepstakes also offer a chance for cross promotion and gaining visibility in markets not normally targeted. For example, if you're a travel agent, you might devise a contest or sweepstake program where the winner gets a gift certificate good at a nearby luggage store. Your promotion can not only be promoted in your office, but in the luggage store as well. And in return, the store providing the gift certificate as the winning gift, will be exposed to the travel agency clients.

Co-op Advertising

see: co-op marketing, cross marketing

Co-op advertising is the sharing of advertising costs by manufacturers, distributors or retail centers. The biggest advantage of co-op advertising is that it saves you money and ultimately stretches your ad budget!

Co-op advertising works with all forms of advertising—that includes print, radio, television, direct mail, billboards and special promotions. An example of co-op advertising is a shoe store ad featuring a specific name brand like Nike or Reebok. The manufacturer may reimburse the store as much as 50 to 100 %, depending on the type of ad and/or the sales generated. Other examples of co-op ads would be a group of individual yogurt shop owners who place an ad that lists several locations throughout an area, or a retail shopping center that places an ad for a holiday special, and in that ad are listed the individual merchants with specific offers. In addition to saving money, co-op advertising adds credibility to your business.

Co-op advertising can also be an acceptable method of generating visibility for professionals, though it may require more creativity on your part! But do some research, it's usually worth your time and energy. For example, if you have an upholstery cleaning service, you may want tie in with a furniture company, or a dietician may want to develop an ad program with a specific organic food or vitamin store. You may find that by including a name and/or logo in your promotional materials, you can receive monetary compensation. Talk with those companies you've targeted, they may have ideas that you hadn't thought about. Be sure to make detailed contractual arrangements.

Tennis Shoe Store

Just Arrived
New Shipment
of *SUPER* Shoes

20 - 30% OFF All Brands
3 Days Only
June 1st - 3rd

ADDRESS

PHONE

This is a sample of a co-op ad provided by the manufacturer for the store.

ABC SHOPPING PLAZA

PRESENTS
The Annual Sidewalk Sale
July 3rd & 4th
Bargains • Bargains • Bargains
At all eight merchants

The Restaurant
2 for 1 Lunch
w/coupon

Stationery Store
Buy 3 cards get
1 FREE w/coupon

The Toy Store
Dozens of 99¢
Summer Toys

- Fish Store
- Grocery Store
- Hair Place
- The Restaurant
- Stationery Store
- Toy Store
- Drug Store
- Coffee Shop

123 1st Street (Between 2nd & 3rd - Downtown)

This is a sample of co-op advertising for locations along with a coupon to track the response.

The

Yogurt Place
100% Natural Yogurt

100 Different Flavors & Toppings
1000's of
possible combinations
10 Locations to serve you

1. _____   2. _____   3. _____

4. _____   5. _____   6. _____

7. _____   8. _____   9. _____

10. _____

Buy One Large, Get A Topping FREE

VALID THROUGH AUGUST 1992

This co-op ad by a group of yogurt shop owners could also double as a flyer.

Coupons

see: mailing lists, door hangers, display ads

Using coupons for your service or product serves two purposes: it brings in new business and identifies the media through which your customers hear about you.

Coupons can be targeted at either bringing in business for a new product/service, or for bringing in new business for old products/services. For instance, you are a restaurant owner who has decided to develop a new breakfast menu. To promote it, you might start by distributing two-for-one breakfast coupons to local residents (either by mail, by door-to-door handouts, or by investing in an ad/coupon in the local newspaper.) In designing your coupon, keep the information concise, clear, and uncluttered. Always include an expiration date, or you could be redeeming the coupon for the next five years (refusing to honor coupons will not endear you to your customers!) Include the name, logo, address, hours of operation, days the coupon is valid and phone number. State whether it is good for one customer/purchase only or for multiple customers/ purchases.

Below is an example of a coupon to introduce a restaurant's new Sunday brunch.

THE BEACH RESTAURANT

INTRODUCES ITS NEW SUNDAY BRUNCH
(with more 100 items to choose from)

$9.95 — ALL YOU CAN ENJOY

BUY ONE BRUNCH AND GET ONE FREE

Located at 111 Ocean Walk, Beach Town
Reservations accepted 555-2222

Valid Sundays only, expires Dec. 31, 1993

Cross-Marketing

see: referral development, telemarketing

Cross-marketing, sometimes called parallel marketing is achieved by promoting your business along with another business that works with, or complements yours, but that does not compete with your business. Cross-marketing goes beyond education to include the offering of a product or service that is closely related to yours.

By providing your customers/clients with this product/service, you accomplish several things: you are providing them with something of value and thereby give them a better perspective of your business; you are creating visibility for yourself or your business in a subtle and active fashion; and you increase your chances of getting a referral or personal recommendation about your business.

An example of a professional service might be a financial planner. Her/his service is fee-based, meaning you pay a set amount for the service you receive. In this case it's advice and a written report outlining your plan of action for financial security. Once you have this plan, your financial consultant may recommend places for you to go to implement the plan. It may be a specific bank for special accounts or a brokerage company to purchase stocks. In return for these recommendations, these companies may in turn recommend the financial planner to their clients seeking comprehensive financial planning, or they may use the planner to give seminars and workshops sponsored by them.

Other examples of cross-marketing could be combining swimwear apparel with sunscreen products or nutritional supplements with a fitness program. With a little thought and creativity, you can come up with some ideas that work for your business as well as the business that you're cross-marketing with.

Often the cross-marketing program will not cost you anything extra, yet will increase the visibility of your marketing campaign.

Customer Appreciation Programs

see: gift certificates, coupons, sales awards & incentives

Your customers want to feel appreciated. Have you ever walked into a store and felt like an annoying interruption for the salespeople? Let your customers know that you realize they are the reason your business exists! This recognition can be simple, such as "We're Glad You're Here!" buttons for restaurant food services. Other examples are: thank-you's printed on the bottom of checks or receipts; "ten percent off on next visit" cards in retail clothing stores; birthday celebrations in restaurants, or mailed birthday cards in professional service industries; free balloons at a stationary store; or "buy 5 get 1 free" cards in a frozen yogurt store; or a thank you note to those who have referred business to you. Customer appreciation programs are often cost-effective ways to keep business coming to you.

Customer Relations

See: customer appreciation programs, public relations, in store displays

Customer relations includes all activities designed to satisfy your customers. This includes customer service, surveys, appreciation programs, quality assurance programs and incentive return programs.

As businesses become more and more competitive, the only way to survive is to provide quality and superior service to your business clientele. Research shows that while 96% of unhappy clients never complain, 90 percent will not return — and each one will tell nine others about their negative experience. It costs five times more to develop new customers than to keep your present ones satisfied and loyal to you.

Customer satisfaction can be measured by looking at the "Three A's": availability, accessibility, and acceptability.

Availability refers to actual types of products/services offered and hours of operation.

Accessibility refers to factors of convenience, such as location, parking, signage, etc.

Acceptability refers to overall satisfaction with your products/services as defined by the consumer.

Remember, your idea of satisfaction may be very different from that of your customers and employees. It is crucial that you regularly survey all of your individual consumer groups so that you meet their particular needs.

The public is quickly turning to comparative shopping for everything they purchase, and what they look for, after quality, is *service*. What does this mean?

1. Fast, courteous service
2. Delivery of what is promised

3. Timely, fair resolution of complaints/problems

4. Consideration and appreciation

A word about employees—if they have direct contact with your customers, they should be instructed to satisfy them before anything else. To get this point across, one restaurant posted a giant sign in the kitchen stating, "Guests Before Egos." Be sure employees are trained to immediately greet customers and to always thank them for their business, to practice correct phone etiquette, and to interact with customers in a professional, courteous manner. However, simply telling them to be "professional and courteous" is not enough. Set specific job descriptions, outlining exact duties/procedures and how they are to be performed (for example, how to answer and direct calls, or how to handle declined credit card). Also, set evaluation criteria in order to have standards against which an employee's performance can be judged. Finally, feedback and rewards are crucial to employee performance. Be sure that service quality is a key element in all performance reviews and that good service is noted and rewarded.

Customer Surveys

see: market research

A short, one-page satisfaction survey distributed to your customers or clients is an excellent way to determine their specific wants and needs. Without such feedback, you may put time and money into activities that produce either no or negative results. Using short, clear sentences and simple words, ask your customers opinions on the friendliness, courteousness and efficiency of your employees. Ask about the quality of your product or service. What would they change about it? How long was their wait? Was parking adequate? How did they find out about your product or service? We've included some sample surveys on the next pages.

If you are really serious about getting these surveys returned, you might consider an inexpensive incentive gift like a single flower for the florist shop or a free cholesterol screening if you are a physician.

Sample: Flower Basket Flower Shop

Dear Customer,

Please fill out the survey below and return it to our cashier. We welcome and value your opinion. It is our aim to provide you with the finest products and service possible! Date of visit _____ Time _____ am/pm

Were our employees courteous and friendly? very 1 2 3 4 5 not at all

Were our employees helpful to you
in selecting your arrangement? very 1 2 3 4 5 not at all

Were the type of flowers you requested in stock? very 1 2 3 4 5 not at all

Were our flowers fresh and in good condition? very 1 2 3 4 5 not at all

What flowers or other products would you like us to carry?

_____

_____

Were our prices reasonable to you? very 1 2 3 4 5 not at all

Was our parking adequate? very 1 2 3 4 5 not at all

Were our store hours convenient to you? very 1 2 3 4 5 not at all

How did you hear about us?

☐ newspaper ad ☐ Yellow Pages ☐ friends ☐ drop-in ☐ other

Would you return?

☐ yes ☐ probably ☐ probably not ☐ no

Would you recommend us to a friend?

☐ yes ☐ probably ☐ probably not ☐ no

Do you have other comments or suggestions that would improve our service to you?

_____

_____

Thank You!

Dear Client:

To reach my goal of providing you with the highest quality health care possible, I ask that you take a few minutes to evaluate my medical practice by filling out the confidential questionnaire below. I appreciate and value your opinions!

—John Doe, MD

Mark the category that most accurately reflects your evaluation of each statement. You may use the space provided on the back of the sheet for additional comments. Please return this form to the receptionist at my office.

Is the office location convenient?	very 1 2 3 4 5 not at all
Are the office hours convenient?	very 1 2 3 4 5 not at all
Is the parking convenient and adequate?	very 1 2 3 4 5 not at all
Is the reception area comfortable, relaxing & clean?	very 1 2 3 4 5 not at all
Is the office staff competent & knowledgeable?	very 1 2 3 4 5 not at all
Is the nursing staff competent & knowledgeable?	very 1 2 3 4 5 not at all
Are all staff members friendly, courteous & caring?	very 1 2 3 4 5 not at all
Are appointment procedures courteous & prompt?	very 1 2 3 4 5 not at all
Are phone calls during office hours handled quickly & efficiently?	very 1 2 3 4 5 not at all
Is the after-hours answering service courteous & prompt?	very 1 2 3 4 5 not at all
When you have an appointment, how do you rank your waiting time?	poor 1 2 3 4 5 excellent
Once you are in the exam room, how do you rank your waiting time?	poor 1 2 3 4 5 excellent
Is your doctor friendly & courteous?	very 1 2 3 4 5 not at all
Does he spend adequate time with you?	very 1 2 3 4 5 not at all
Does he explain the reason for tests & procedures satisfactorily?	poor 1 2 3 4 5 excellent
Do you feel comfortable questioning him?	very 1 2 3 4 5 not at all
Do you feel he is knowledgeable & competent?	very 1 2 3 4 5 not at all
Do you think our fees are fair & reasonable?	very 1 2 3 4 5 not at all
Has your billing been accurate, efficient and timely?	very 1 2 3 4 5 not at all
Do you receive adequate help with your insurance claims?	very 1 2 3 4 5 not at all

THANKS —- We appreciate your input!

Data Bases/Mailing Lists

see: direct response advertising, direct mail, catalogs

Along with the advent of the computer came the formation of data bases which contain information on almost every subject and individual. Your local library should have the names of data bases available to your type of business. There are numerous directories of mailing lists and data bases. Please ask your local reference librarian for help in developing a list for your own business. Once you locate them, it's usually a matter of contacting them for additional information.

Mailing houses often also act as list brokers and/or will refer you to companies specializing in developing mailing lists. Always ask about error rates (they should be no more than 20%), how their data are collected, how often the information is updated and the type of clients they serve. Don't be afraid to shop around, costs vary depending on how large and specific or segmented you want your list. For example, you could buy lists of:

- the residents in your county

- the small businesses in your zip code

- flower shops in Manhattan

- subscribers to *Inc.* magazine

- home owners in your county who make more than $40,000 per year.

- gift purchasers who spent over $200 with a large national catalog

In general, the more specific the list, the more it will cost, and probably the better it will work. Before plunging into large lists and mailing, you should read some of the terrific books on the subject, or consult an expert.

Probably the most important thing you can do in this area is to develop your own data base for your use. From the beginning, start collecting and organizing data on your customers, clients, referral sources and prospective clients. Knowing as much as you can about these important people will enable you to serve their needs effectively and efficiently. Gather all marketing and advertising results and use this information to make future decisions. This information can also be used to develop a targeted mailing list for future mailings. Remember, your current users are far more likely to buy another product from you (assuming they're satisfied) than are people unfamiliar with your products.

Demonstrations

see: trade shows, fairs, in-store promotions

When introducing a new product, it is often difficult to sell it well unless customers can either see it tested (they know what it's for, and they know it works) or try it for themselves. Demonstrations are a great method to gain attention. They can be set up at state or regional fairs, in retail and specialty stores and at trade shows for business-related products and services.

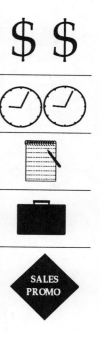

Directories

see: Yellow Pages, display ads, classified ads

In addition to the Yellow Pages, dozens of other special directories are published each year. Some are designed for specific communities, some are produced by professional organizations and clubs, while others compete directly with the Yellow Pages.

There is a big difference between directory ads and print media ads. When people refer to a directory, they are ready to buy and are looking for the service they need. They do not have to be persuaded to buy—only convinced to buy from you! Directory advertising is appropriate for nearly all types of small businesses.

If more than one directory is distributed in your area, find out which are the most used and widely read. Ask around, contact other merchants in your area if you are a retailer, other professionals if it's a service you offer and then check your home or office for the ones you are currently using.

When deciding if you should be listed in a specific directory, ask yourself the following questions.

*   How long has the directory been in business?

*   Is the directory complete—does it have enough information to be useful to many people?

*   How many people does it reach and how is it distributed?

*   Is the publication well organized, easy to understand and cross-referenced?

The directory's representatives can provide you with answers to many of these questions and other information in terms of who uses their books and their frequency of use. But remember, they are also there to sell ads, so a little research on your part will be worth it.

For targeted markets, contact trade and professional organizations that are relevant to your business. Often for the price of a membership you will receive a listing in its directory. Others may offer the opportunity to just buy an ad or listing in the directory. Don't forget to include any social clubs. These directories are often trusted by the membership when shopping for a service or product, especially if they are new members, or new to the area.

Make your sublisting/category selections carefully. Not only can multiple listings get expensive, but you can waste time responding to inquiries which are not productive because of the directories' frequent use!

Having listings in many local directories is a good way to increase visibility and name recognition, but it can also be expensive and money wasted if it doesn't reach your desired audience.

Below is an example of a simple directory listing. Sample #7, on the next page, shows two display ads which can be used in directories.

Johnson Accounting & Associates
555 Main St., Ste. 100...000-0000

SMITH COLLECTIBLES

We Buy & Sell
- Estate Jewelry
- Sterling Silver
- Ivory
- Jade

Appraisal & Auctions
Since 1920

000-0000
7777 East Main • Santa Ana, CA

Dunn Antiques

444 West Central
321-234-5555

PROFESSIONAL ESTATE SALE SERVICES

- Single Items
- Entire Estates Purchased

Specializing in Fine
Furniture, China,
Vintage Clothing,
Dolls & Silver

In Business Since 1959

A simple display ad without a logo and one with a logo

Direct Mail

see: door hangers, flyers/inserts, newsletters, packaging, data bases

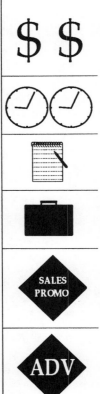

Direct mail is an increasingly popular strategy that involves mailing letters, brochures or other advertising materials to potential clients. This tactic gives you a great degree of control and flexibility over who receives your message, as well as the content of the message. But in order to be successful with direct mail programs you must rely on very specialized mailing lists to reach very targeted groups. That means you must carefully select the audience based on buying habits, age, income, occupation, zip code, etc.

Direct mail works best for businesses offering a tangible product or service. If your business has neither, try to have a call to action by offering something free such as a booklet or consultation so that you can get a response to your mail piece.

The best direct mail piece provides an attractive offer that the recipient can reply to. Additionally, you can use personal letters and pamphlets to communicate your expertise and the benefits you can offer an individual. But be sure to include some way to track a response, either with a tear off coupon, or a response card that can be mailed back.

This type of communication is also good for keeping-in-touch mailings, reminding customers and clients you exist, building accurate mailing lists for future promotions, image building by keeping your name in front of the public, and advertising. (Newsletters also work as direct mail pieces because they are a good way of making contact with prospects and referral sources on a regular basis.) A direct mail piece provides detailed information to the reader and is a tangible representation of your business. Direct mail can and should be very personalized to the needs and desires of your targeted audience. You can also determine almost immediately if your piece was a success or a failure. As a general rule, you can usually expect 15% of the total responses within the first week of mailing, and an overall 5% response rate is respectable. Often follow-up mailings are done after the initial one, to further increase your response rate. The most challenging aspect of this strategy is creating a piece that gets your audience to respond.

Another way to evaluate if a direct mail campaign is right for your business is to look at how much copy and illustration you need to sell your product or service. If you need a lot then direct mail is probably the best. Also consider the price; generally, if the product doesn't have at least a $15 profit margin at a $29.95 retail price, chances are you will not be successful in a solo mailing, unless it's an incredible product or service.

When you price your item/service, it must be perceived as a value. Value/price is different in every market—what one market perceives as value, can be viewed as cheap in another. Again, that goes back to knowing your market's income, needs and buying patterns which was established through research and past experiences.

The price of an item and the market will determine the media selection you choose. But also you'll need to consider your budget, that often dictates the quantity/circulation, type of mailing lists, when to launch, any seasonal considerations, and the size of an advertising schedule.

Once you've nailed down a budget, the market and the kind of media program, you can begin to design the selling materials. These may be in the form of a personal letter, a brochure, or some other type of mail piece. The designing of collateral material will be crucial to your business, because they sets the tone and image of your company. That image must appeal to your market and that market must perceive your company as a qualified source for what you're offering. A business selling jewelry will have a very different look from one selling children's clothing.

Here are few other ideas to help increase the effectiveness of your program.

- Create a special introductory price for first time customers.

- Offer a bonus gift or premium for prompt orders.

- Make people feel they'll be the first to get a product/ service.

- Provide discounts to loyal customers on their next purchase.

- Use special pricing such as "for a limited time only."

- Guarantee the offer.

- Include testimonials.

- Include a tangible object in your mailing, a postage stamp or pen, etc. to create more visibility.

- Make your package simple and mistake proof.

- Have a call to action!

- Get feedback on your packages, test your offer and track your response from both mailing lists and promotional offers.

A direct mail program must be well-planned and managed. There are high costs involved in developing materials, paying for copywriting, graphics, printing, mailing lists and postage. However, if you look at it on a per-sale basis it is often the least expensive method of marketing. Even with targeted lists and careful planning, the response rate can be low. Using direct mail in conjunction with telemarketing increases response rates. If you consider bulk rate mail to keep costs down, also consider how it would effect your program if it was never delivered or if it was delivered late. This is a serious concern and problem for dated materials. Last but not least, remember you are competing with an increasing amount of direct mail cluttering mailboxes and it's that much more important that your promotional piece be noticed.

Grabbing the reader's attention, sparking interest and desire and encouraging action, is the intent and purpose of a direct mail piece's written copy. Look for a dramatic opening and speak to the reader in a personal way. Lengthy copy is okay as long as you are specific and include facts. It's important to involve the reader and get them to act now—include an offer, an expiration date and an easy and convenient way for them to respond.

If you are packaging a direct mail piece, your goal is to get the piece noticed and opened whether it comes in an envelope or is a self mailer. The outer portion is very important. There are several ways to accomplish this.

1. Use phrases that say free, introductory offer or that promise an important benefit.

2. Use colors and graphic design to make it visually interesting and valuable.

3. Create mystery and/or curiosity to pique the reader's interest in opening it.

4. List the features offered that will benefit the buyer.

Don't ignore the envelope or self-mailer portion—it's often more important than the content. This is what may get the person to actually open your piece. Addresses should be typed and a teaser such as "valuable offer inside, or free give-away, see details inside," should be visible. When using color, graphics and other details on the envelope let the nature of your offer and the targeted audience be the guide. For example if you are targeting a highly professional audience, your mailer should be more upscale, using quality paper stock and color ink. But if the mailer is going to an entire zip code area, the production of the piece need not be as elaborate. The idea is to create a piece that talks to your audience For that reason, it is important that you know and understand the most salient characteristics of your audience.

Whole books have been written on the subject of direct mail. If you plan to use direct mail as part of your marketing mix, use your library or visit a bookstore to get more familiar with the planning and execution of a successful direct mail campaign.

A further word of caution—if you choose a direct mail campaign, do your homework. Make sure you have good mailing lists and know the market you want to reach, give thought to the layout of your piece and enlist the help of a graphic designer. You may even want to consult a direct mail expert. As cost effective as this tool can be, it can be a waste of money if it's not done properly.

Direct Response Advertising

see: mail order, catalogs, direct mail

The definition of direct response advertising is—selling to people identified by name, address or buying habits, the product is convenient to get to such as mailed directly, the ads are used to make an immediate order/sale or create a response, the ads use repetition, stressing key points, more than once in the body of your copy, and the consumer perceives a risk because the product is purchased unseen.

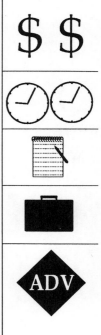

The three elements of direct response advertising are a definite offer, all the necessary information to make a decision and a simple way to respond, for example a response card or number to call.

This marketing tool is appropriate if you're trying to renew subscriptions to a newsletter business, have a service where you provide quotes to gain work, want to reach charity donors or association members. It's also an ideal tool to sell products that cannot be gotten through retail outlets.

The advantages of direct response advertising are several. You'll get a measurable response, both in its costs and in its income, it's pretty much guaranteed to reach the selected audience, it can be followed up with telemarketing and there are very few restrictions on how it will look. A direct mail package can include response cards, specialty items, letters, brochures, etc. When compared to other mediums, this one offers a lot more flexibility.

Display Advertising

see: classified ads, inserts, direct mail

Display advertising accounts for the majority of the ad space in newspapers and magazines and for the majority of their revenues. The retail businesses have the most to benefit from this type of advertising because they're the ones with specific events such as holiday sales, grand openings and weekly specials. Display ads are also run on a regular basis, and are vital in maintaining visibility within a targeted market. Display advertising can be very costly ...and the larger the publication's readership, the more it will cost to reach them.

Generally speaking, professionals are wiser to spend their time and money in other ways because display advertising will probably not generate results equivalent to the amount of effort and money you must invest. However, if you choose this marketing tool you'll want to target your community newspapers or perhaps specific sections in the major papers such as health, travel or business sections.

Developing a display advertisement requires more knowledge and preparation than a classified ad. Most display ads contain headlines, copy and graphics and some sort of call to action, such as a phone number to call, or a redeemable coupon.

Some publications include the cost of designing and developing an ad in the cost of advertising, but others may charge you a production fee. You can have an ad designed for your business by your printer or through desktop publishing at a fairly reasonable rate. Designing your own ad with the help of a professional can also give you more flexibility in what you do with your ad space in terms of layout and design. Once you have an ad that works for your business you can use it over and over again, saving money in the long run.

On the following pages are fictitious samples to show you different concepts. These ads do not represent any actual companies.

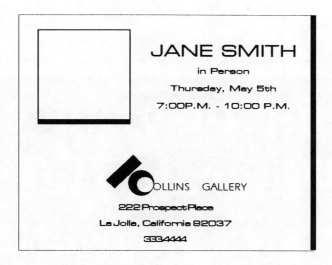

This is a sample of a display ad for a gallery that is exhibiting a new artist. This ad displays a picture of the artist's work, a gallery logo and information on the opening.

Rogers & Rogers

The CPA Firm for Small Business

**Call us for a FREE
Brochure on Running
A Small Business**

555-5555
8888 Prospect Ave. • La Jolla, CA 92037

- **Tax Planning**
- **Bookkeeping**
- **Financial Management**
- **Computer Consulting**
- **Auditing**

This is a sample of a display ad for a professional service. The CPA firm specializes in small businesses and also offers to send their free brochure.

Our Insurance Program Has You Covered!

If you need insurance for personal or professional needs, the Small Business Society offers plans to give you comprehensive coverage.

For Information Call
Your Local Representative at:

555-0000

We will send you our FREE Brochure highlighting our programs.

COVERED INSURANCE
P.O. BOX 000
NEW YORK, NY

This display ad is an example of business-to-business marketing, in this case an insurance company offering coverage to members of The California Small Business Society.

Door Hangers

see: flyers inserts, coupons, direct mail

Door hangers are a very effective way to reach an area close to your business. Because they are hand delivered, you know exactly who gets them. This form of advertising is very inexpensive, especially if you deliver the hangers yourself. If done this way, you only have layout and printing costs. If you don't have the time, find students and pay them! It still won't cost you too much.

Door hangers can be a good marketing tool for Realtors and small businesses providing services such as landscaping or cleaning, retail businesses and restaurants. Door hangers should always have some kind of call to action, perhaps the offer of a discount, a free demonstration, or a free product with purchase of another. The coupons make it easier to track response, thereby allowing you to gauge the success of your efforts.

Hangers can be used to introduce a new business in the area, a new product or expanded service for an existing business.

Depending on what it is you're offering, once you have a layout, your door hangers can be reprinted and redelivered. Just be sure to change the expiration date if you've used a coupon.

SALES PROMO

Educational Programs

see: seminars, conferences, writing articles, trade shows

Making the public aware of you and your business will be very difficult if they are not already aware of the "bigger picture" in which you play a part. Sometimes you must educate your consumers about your particular field before you can educate them specifically about your expertise or product. Some initial research into the public's level of awareness might be warranted to get answers to questions such as: Do they know what my service is or does? Do they understand the importance of my service? Then, once some broader understanding is achieved, it will be much easier to successfully implement marketing strategies that promote your specific business expertise.

Education works well as a marketing strategy, because it appears to offer "something for nothing." Offering a free seminar on a timely topic, or writing an informative article in your newsletter or sponsoring a community event will create the impression that you care enough about what you're doing to volunteer information to help the public. Since you do care, it is a very powerful marketing tool.

Costs will vary depending on whether you will be self-promoting and incurring the expense of renting a room, serving food and running an ad campaign to support your own programs. This can be a high risk venture compared to having an organization absorb these costs as part of their on-going educational programs. The goal of these educational PR/media relations tools is to position yourself as an expert in the industry and to position your company as the source people automatically turn to for the service/product. You may want to begin your efforts in this area by co-sponsoring or developing events with local organizations.

Fairs (Regional and State)

see: demonstrations, trade shows

Every year thousands of people attend fairs just to see the latest products and newest inventions that make life's chores a little easier. Regional and/or state fairs can be an excellent place to demonstrate and sell products. Fairs provide an audience looking to buy gadgets and gizmos as well as a built-in repeat customer business. This group is also a very loyal following and they make an effort to find you. Generally speaking this market is looking for items that can't be found in the stores: gadgets that save time, are a good value for the money or are replenishing their products from previous years.

Some product categories are particularly viable for this kind of selling: household care products, or lawn and garden, or automotive products are excellent candidates for exhibiting at fairs. Because part of the selling process at fairs is being able to put on a good show, be sure that whoever is in your booth selling, knows the product well, can demonstrate it efficiently and is outgoing and friendly.

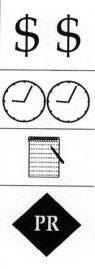

Gift Certificates

see: coupons

Gift certificates are a wonderful marketing tool for retail businesses like salons, gift shops, restaurants, record, clothing stores or fitness centers.

Gift certificates differ from coupons because the certificates are paid for by the person who buys it to give as a gift.

Gift certificates work on the same premise as word of mouth...since it's an already satisfied customers who buys the certificate to give to another. Not only are they telling another, but they've paid for whatever it is your business offers. Gift certificates can introduce potential customers who are not already familiar with your product or service. Another way to use them is to give them to unsatisfied customers as way to get them to come back and give your business a second chance. But don't confuse gift certificates with coupons. Gift certificates are usually purchased in $5, $10 or $20 increments and don't usually put any kind of limits on the user. Coupons usually do, either by giving a discount, offering a two-for-one or valid only on certain days or hours.

When creating gift certificates, if rules apply make sure they are clear. Rules usually refer to the cash redemption policy and whether they can be redeemed for cash or only business credit.

The only costs in setting up gift certificates, is having them designed and printed. In doing so, make sure they cannot be duplicated. This usually means only a few people can authorize and sign them. Since they may be redeemable for cash, you should treat them carefully and use some type of numbering system for each gift certificate with a log sheet detailing each purchase.

Grand Openings

see: in-store displays

A grand opening is designed to draw attention and create excitement for your new business. It can also be the first step in the foundation on which you build a prosperous business. This marketing tool works best for retail businesses of all types, including restaurants.

In planning your event, consider the best way to display your merchandise and highlight your services. For example, a crafts business would feature demonstrations using its products, or a medical clinic may offer complimentary health screening. Pay attention to the details...are balloons appropriate to create a festive atmosphere, should you feature a special guest, or an animated character for children, are coupons or gift certificates feasible to encourage repeat customers while you build your niche, or does it make sense to hold a drawing. There are lots of ways to encourage your new customers (and even local media) to attend, so spend time developing a terrific program appropriate to your audience.

You get only one chance to make a first impression—be sure you are ready.

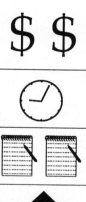

Grand Openings to Benefit Charities

For some businesses, such as an upscale restaurant or an art gallery opening, a charity benefit works well. The key in this kind of opening is finding a charity that fits with your image and demographics. The advantage in sponsoring an event for charity is that it's easy to generate free press coverage for your sponsored event through press releases and Public Service Announcements. For this kind of opening, an admission price/donation is collected and the proceeds go to the designated charity. The bulk of your mailing list for the event comes from the charity, but also included are your vendors, business associates and friends.

Don't forget to have a guest book on-hand for your guests to sign-in. This will be the beginning of your mailing list/database for future sales, events and promotional announcements.

Publicizing your event can be accomplished through many different avenues. To start the ball rolling, send a press release to the appropriate press. This is especially applicable where you're offering the public something for free, or are organizing a charity benefit. If your location is part of an existing shopping center, try to tie in with them. You may also consider newspaper, radio & television advertising, direct mail, door-to-door, co-op advertising and co-promotion.

An Open House

Professionals such as attorneys, accountants, health care professionals and business consultants would be better served by sending formal announcements of the new practice/office and holding an open house. This is considered a low-key type of marketing tool and is more appropriate to professional practices. Ideally an open house is scheduled after working hours and provides hors d'oeuvres with beverages and/or cocktails. It is smaller in scope with a more personal touch. Invitations should be sent to current clients, referral sources, business associates and friends. At the time of the open house, be sure new business cards and brochures (when appropriate) are displayed in prominent locations and are available for the taking.

If a grand opening or an open house is not appropriate, you may want to consider using specialty items like note pads, phone stickers or calendars which can be sent by direct mail or delivered door-to-door. This type of announcement can be used by a real estate agent or other type of sales person who has been hired by an existing office.

Identity/Image of Your Business

see: business cards, stationery, collateral
materials

The image of your business should be determined and controlled by you. An image should be built around the characteristics you are proud of, whether it be quality products, personal attention or customer satisfaction. If you're having a hard time finding anything unique about your business, then create something that makes you different. It will be the unique features that allow you to compete on your own terms, especially against the more established, larger, similar businesses.

Everything you do will add to building your image—that includes how you do business, the type of advertising done, your business cards, stationery and collateral materials.

If you don't consciously determine your image, chances are one will be created anyway...and if it's not the one you want, you can have an expensive and difficult time changing it.

Look at the unique strengths that your business has and build on those. There are surprisingly many advantages to using small businesses for your clients and you must determine which of those appeal to your market and build around them. Let's take as an example an independent contractor with an architectural background who specializes in kitchen remodeling. He cannot compete with a large construction company on pricing. No matter how he tries, his job will undoubtedly cost more. But in return for the higher price, his clients know they will receive more attention to the finished look of the design, a better grade of materials, personal service, satisfaction, and a finished project on-time and on budget. For this type of service many people are willing to pay a little extra. So instead of emphasizing costs, all of his advertising and collateral materials stress quality craftsmanship, attention to details and client satisfaction.

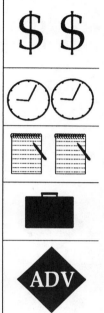

Inserts/Flyers

see: advertising, direct mail

Inserts/flyers are specifically designed advertising pieces that are placed (inserted) into carrying vehicles, for example, newspapers, magazines, or newsletters. Inserts can be a cost effective way of reaching large markets because you don't have the costs of mailing lists and postage. You are only paying for printing and insertion fees. Like the vehicle carrying them, inserts/flyers can reach highly targeted audiences.

Inserts/flyers provide as much copy space as needed, have a lot of flexibility in format and can be inserted into other publications whether they be newspapers, trade journals or magazines. They can be as simple as a one-color, one-page flyer announcing a free financial seminar, or they can be a two-color brochure with a response card, or as elaborate, as a four-page, full color piece showing homes in an area for sale.

Inserts in daily newspapers can be difficult because of your many options and the readers' reading habits. Be sure to ask your newspaper advertising sales representative which days and which sections will best reach your target market. With most publications, the daily circulation and readership varies (as does the cost of inserting). If you have a special event happening, you'll want to be sure your insert is included in the right section on the right day.

Magazines are similarly structured. Editorial calendars which dictate the content of the issues, are planned six months to a year in advance. In addition to the regular editorial, specific themes are planned to which you may want to tie your product.

In-Store Displays

see: sales promotion, radio, television, display ads

In-store displays, often referred to as point of purchase (POP) displays, are another form of promotion. POP displays can be special racks, signs, banners, and exhibits. They are common in retail stores to support the sales or increase awareness for a designated product or service. POP displays have become increasing popular because of a trend toward self-service. And what better way to draw attention to merchandise than with a sign or exhibit.

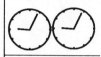

POP promotions are also used to remind people that a product is available at the location, to influence the purchase of a specific name product, and to encourage impulse buying. Nightclubs use neon liquor signs and interior designers display signs for fabric cleaners and protector products.

It is not uncommon for prime or additional retail space to be paid for by the business that wants the sign or items displayed. In other words, be aware that if you develop a strong POP display, you may still have to pay the store for the privilege of displaying it in a prime location. Sometimes with a proven, successful display, the retailer will pay for the POP materials.

SALES PROMO

Manufacturers often wonder why retailers don't use their POP materials. In some cases, retailers won't display POP material because they don't want to show favoritism. But more often it is because the displays don't fit the retailer's needs, the materials are inferior looking, the program is presented by an unprofessional sales person or there just isn't enough profit in the product. If you are a retailer, POP displays can help you segment your space efficiently and draw buyers from one part of the store to another. They are an important part of your in-store merchandising. If you are a manufacturer, you may want to look at how your competitors are using POP to more effectively market their products in-store.

Mail Order

see: catalogs, direct response advertising, direct mail

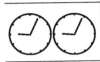

Knowing how to evaluate a product/service to find a niche is a key to being successful in the business of mail order.

In a mail order business one of the most important elements is knowing to whom you are trying to sell to. Do the research to get a good profile of your typical customer or the customer you want to reach. Know the demographics (age, sex, income level) and psychographics (attitudes, buying habits, opinions, etc.) From this information you will know what type of mailing lists to develop and purchase. Knowing your market intimately will also help you in developing new products and offering new services down the road.

Just as important as knowing your customers, is knowing how to reach them. Your mailing list is your only means of talking to your market, so know how your list was developed. For example, if your business is selling seeds and flower bulbs, you may want to consider the following types of lists:

- Homeowners in specific neighborhoods or states

- People who have purchased garden tools or products in the past year

- Subscribers to a gardening magazine

- People who have purchased gardening supplies from other catalogs

Anyone in mail order will tell you that the mailing list you use is a large part of the success of your direct mail program. For that reason, most experts in the field suggest you TEST, TEST, TEST. Buy smaller quantities of an appropriate mailing list, and test the program. See how it works. You can always then increase the size of your mailing program. But testing a list also allows you to get rid of lists that aren't going to work for you at an early stage.

The real advantage of developing a solid mail order customer base occurs as you expand your business. If you have a thriving mail order seeds and bulbs business, when you decide to expand into fertilizers, planters and outdoor furniture, your current list is an appropriate market. Plus your market already knows your name and hopefully your good reputation for delivering quality.

Marketing Budgets

see: Marketing Communications Calendar

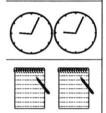

It is important that you define for yourself how much money you are willing to spend on marketing. Many businesses choose to spend some set percentage of their sales on their marketing programs. Usually start-up businesses focus on more time-consuming but less expensive marketing programs. As your business grows and the dollars involved grow, you can afford to spend more to continue building your business.

Whatever stage you are at currently, however, we recommmend you having a comprehensive annual marketing budget listing all of the monies spent on marketing efforts. A quarterly review of the success of these efforts should be part of your planning process.

A Few Budgeting Tips

When you are creating your promotional budget, keep the following in mind.

- *Set objective and priorities.* There's never enough money to do it all, especially with new businesses.

- *Give yourself some flexibility.* A budget is a tool to help control your expenses. Don't be afraid to change a strategy if there's a new opportunity. You can't predict a sluggish economy, a chance to promote a new product or the opportunity to take advantage of a competitor that goes out of business.

- *Use a calendar.* Set budgets according to time, yearly, quarterly, monthly and/or by markets and products.

- *Expect the unexpected.* Set aside some money for the unexpected.

- *Spend money to make money.* You can't sell a product or service if no one knows about it.

Marketing Communication Calendar

see: display advertising, classified ads, radio, television, cable, billboards, direct mail

Once you have chosen the media and marketing vehicles to enhance your business, you will need to organize them in an orderly and logical manner. That means getting a master calendar and indicating weekly, monthly, or annually the media in which you have ads running and specifications (for example, size if it is print, dates and times if it's electronic, etc.) Also include any special sales or promotions. Your calendar should also note the specific you are targeting. This is very simple, but important. All you need is a calendar. Either buy one or make one, and then block-off your planned activities and write down the information. As a "marketing program at a glance" it will enable you to plan your time and finances, make advance arrangements for special promotions, holidays or slow periods and prevents lapses in activity. Your calendar should include the marketing tactics used during each month of the year, or, at a minimum, the quarter, their duration and cost. Keeping track of your program will help you in planning the coming year as well as determining which programs gave you the best response and which were not cost effective.

In planning your marketing calendar, there are several items you should keep in mind.

1. Does your budget (monthly/quarterly) have allowances for production costs?

2. Do your media buys give you enough reach and frequency to make an impact on your target market?

3. Have you set aside a reserve fund for special opportunities that come up or for emergencies?

4. Can you qualify for any bulk rates, or discounted prices?

For an effective media and marketing calendar you must purchase your ads in a way that reaches a large share of your targeted markets and that gives you frequency so you can build awareness for your business.

In selecting your media, look at each possible vehicle's demographics (age, income, etc.) and psychographics (lifestyle & buy-

MAY MEDIA SCHEDULE

SUNDAY	MONDAY	TUESDAY	WEDNESDAY	THURSDAY	FRIDAY	SATURDAY
MAY MEDIA SCHEDULE	**Clothing Store** • Budget • Special Promotions	- radio station $1,500 - print ads -$1,800 - Mother's Day, Memorial Weekend Summer Sale	**1**	**2**	**3** Monthly Womens Magazine $500 1/4 page	**4**
5	**6** Radio Schedule Mother's Day Promotion *emphasis - special gifts under $30	**7** :60 spots @ 7:30 am	**8** :60 spots @ 7:30 am 2:30 pm 6:00 pm The Tribune $400 1/4 page Lifestyle Section	**9** :60 spots @ 7:30 am 2:30 pm 6:00 pm The Reader $150 Co-op 1/2 page w/shopping center	**10** :60 spots 8:30 am 2:30 pm 6:00 pm 9:00 pm	**11** :60 spots @ 8:30 am, 2:30 pm 6:00 & 9:00 pm The Tribune $250 1/2 pg Co-op w/center 1/2 pg lifestyle sec.
12 MOTHER'S DAY	**13**	**14**	**15**	**16**	**17**	**18**
19	**20**	**21**	**22**	**23** The Tribune 1/4 page ad $400 *emphasis summer sale	**24** local Community Publication 1/4 pg $100 *emphasis summer sale	**25**
26	**27**	**28**	**29**	**30** Radio: giveaway coupons = free mentions throughout weekend	**31**	

MEMORIAL WEEKEND

ing habits) to make sure it is geared to the market you want to reach. Also scrutinize the geographic area reached to insure you are reaching the audience you want.

Use your marketing communication calendar as a single, fully-integrated center to track all marketing activity and/or programs being run by your company. Review last year's calendar, and the value of each program, before committing again to a program. Be sure each of your employees, particularly those that have any contact with customers, is aware of programs being run. You might even circulate an employee or company wide version of the calendar and ask for feedback and suggestions.

Media Relations

see: public relations, publicity, press release

Good media relations result in publicity for your business—that is free publicity that can be generated by any of the print or electronic media.

In order to gain free coverage you must get the attention of the editors and writers. You can usually gain attention by creating a special event, getting involved in civic or charity events, providing community service, sponsoring an educational program or identifying trends that relate to your business. Once you've got the vehicle, you must notify the appropriate press of what you're planning or what your business is doing by sending out a press release.

Many small business owners think of media relations as front page stories and photographs featuring their business or product. But media relations also includes free coverage for a variety of other items.

Employee news—hiring a new employee or awarding a promotion. This is usually of interest to local business publications or community papers, whether it's the town where an employee resides or one where the company is located. These publications want to know what is happening in the community they serve.

Customer news—you can get coverage if you have a celebrity who frequents your business/buys your product, a customer who travels an unusual distance, or a customer that has come-up with a use other than that for which the product was intended. Again, it's all in the way it's presented...the more creatively it's done, the better your chance of receiving coverage.

Unique service—in addition to your traditional services, have you been able to fulfill a customer's unusual request?

As the owner—is your background different or unusual, are you a noted speaker, have you received awards that might warrant a story?

The key in generating free publicity is to be creative and try to find a unique angle. Notify the appropriate editors and writers, and then follow up, follow up, follow up.

Networking Through Associations

see: community involvement, referrals, education, peer group marketing, public speaking

Almost every field has a professional association or organization and these types of groups provide excellent opportunities for you to network. Membership will increase your visibility and enhance your reputation.

Organizations are excellent places to get referrals and even to establish joint ventures or collaborations. Associations also provide regular meetings, social events, publications and education programs of which you can take advantage. The only costs are your time and your membership dues.

In addition to professional associations, civic, religious and social groups can also be valuable places to meet people in your community and to let them know you are there to serve them.

To get involved in these types of groups you may want to give a luncheon speech to a local trade organizations like the Rotarians on some interesting aspect of your profession or business, or offer to conduct a group discussion related to your specialty at the local church—these kinds of activities educate the public and make your name and services visible. And of course you are also building credibility as a speaker for larger events such as seminars, workshops and sponsored courses.

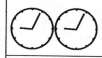

Newsletters

see: articles for publication, direct mail

Producing a newsletter offers many advantages. Newsletters can quickly build an image, increase visibility, establish a reputation, and provide the vehicle to be viewed as an expert. Writing and publishing a newsletter, however, is no small task, but can serve as an excellent way to communicate with current, existing and potential business. When designed properly, they offer interesting and valuable information.

Newsletters are also a good forum to test new ideas and receive feedback. They are typically one to eight pages long and contain brief articles that focus on a market's specific needs or interests.

The information for each of your issues can be derived from a variety of sources. Newspapers, trade publications, magazines, and journals can all be good sources for article ideas. The concept for your newsletter should be to have informative and interesting material to educate your market. Consider having a different "theme" for each issue to cover the spectrum of topics in your industry and the variety of clients in your business. You can use the space to discuss changes in your services or staff, a special offer for new clients/patrons, seminars you offer and, of course, to promote your expertise. But since this is viewed as an educational vehicle avoid blowing your own horn too obviously.

Newsletters work well for businesses or professionals in areas that have a constant flow of new information, whether it is lifestyle trends, small business practices, or the ever-changing tax regulations.

While most newsletters are distributed at no charge, others carry a subscription fee and produce revenue. For most professionals, a free publication is no doubt the most appropriate.

Newsletters are best published on a regular basis which conveys dependability and commitment. At a minimum, publish on a quarterly basis. If your budget allows for a bimonthly or monthly newsletter, that's even better because one of the key reasons for the newsletter is to keep your name in front of your targeted market. You would probably be better off sending out a two-page newsletter every month rather than an eight-page newsletter every quarter.

Costs, in both time and money, can be a major deterrent to newsletter publishing. It isn't cheap to write, design, print and mail a new issue to hundreds of customers and potential customers every few months.

Here are some ways to cut corners. Consider using a qualified graphic designer to design and prepare your camera-ready art. You can prepare the articles on your computer and hand over the disk, saving money on production. Further, you could use a copy shop with a high quality copier for printing and folding. The results will still be professional-looking but it won't break your budget. If your newsletter becomes a significant marketing program, you might consider two-color printing once it is well established.

The first issue should be sent to your database of current customers and those groups you have identified as referral sources or prospective business (see database). You should continually build your mailing list to include new contacts made through referrals, networking and other marketing activities. If your list is not large enough, you can buy targeted lists from companies that sell them.

Mailing lists are not very expensive to purchase, but using your own list costs nothing and is more likely to ensure you reach the right people. If your database is small, 100-200, you can handle the mailing yourself using first-class postage. As it grows much beyond that, consider getting a bulk rate postage permit or using a mailing house.

Packaging

see: Identity/Image of your business

"Packaging" a business whether that business is selling a product or a service can be the "make-or-break" difference. More and more we are discovering that how a product/service is packaged and presented will directly affect its sales.

"Packaging" refers to the way your business presents itself to prospective customers, users, vendors and employees. The term comes from product marketing in which managers are directly concerned with the physical presentation of the product, or the package. In product marketing, they talk about packaging as the physical box that surrounds the corn flakes. Creating a package for corn flakes involves defining a target audience, developing the right copy and visuals, finding the perfect name, providing the proper labeling and much more.

Today, the term has been extended to more broadly define the way businesses present themselves and their products or services to the world. When you evaluate your "packaging," you are looking at it from the outside in. How well is your product presented to its intended audience? If its a fun, lively, engaging product, is that product concept reflected in the product's design, signage, P-O-P displays, advertising, direct mail, PR, etc. On the other hand, if you are selling a serious, competent, professional service, have you packaged all of the elements of the service and the image to talk directly to the needs of your intended audience.

You need to consider just how your packaging talks to the buyer— is it easy to recognize and identify, does it have a clear message as to its features and benefits, will it actually sell the product and is the packaging consistent with the content and price.

In order to evaluate your "packaging," think broadly. Like a product manager, first begin by defining your intended audience (or target audience). What do you know about them? What are you trying to sell to them? If you are trying to sell use of a store, you are going to have to think differently about packaging then if you are trying to develop a practice or trying to sell a product. In each case

though begin with your target. Define as many of their characteristics as you can. If you don't know much about them, do some
research. Examine your assumptions. Now take a look at how well
what you are trying to sell is packaged for its intended audience.

Peer Group Marketing

see: cross-marketing, sales/referral development

Peer group marketing relates back to associations and networking, and stresses the importance of getting together with peers. However, beyond simply getting out there and shaking hands, peer group marketing emphasizes the importance of telling those people who have the power to refer clients to you about your business.

You need to understand your role as part of a group of peers in your field and make effective use of that role—all of us have unique contributions to make. The key to peer-based marketing is to have well-known people in your community participate constructively in your business. If you can do this, you will generate personal recommendations and undoubtedly a substantial amount of business.

Often your friends and associates will be happy to help out, but in some cases it is appropriate to pay an honorarium or compensate them in some other way. Consider inviting your peers to a luncheon "brainstorming" session addressing your business (remember to pick up the check), to an office reception or ask them to give presentations to your clients on an issue related to them. They can also participate in any seminars and workshops that you produce.

Personal Letters

see: Personal recommendations, direct mail

One of the easiest and most effective marketing tools is the personal letter. They are perfectly suited to professionals and service businesses. All you need is a clearly written letter that uses proper spelling and grammar. The letter should highlight your business and what you are offering the reader (for example, a free demonstration or estimate.) This type of letter enables you to convey a sincere personal feeling, especially if you include personal data on the reader (for example, things such as their business, home, or purchasing habits.) Of course you must first learn about your prospective clients, whether it is through library research, questionnaires, observation, referrals or your own database of information.

You can increase the effectiveness of your personal letter by writing a brief follow up letter or making a phone call within two weeks of the original. Through the course of the letter and phone conversation you are building a relationship, not only with potential clients but with potential referral sources. Try to avoid simply inserting each person's name in predetermined places in a generic letter. Instead compose each letter separately, and strive to include as many specific personal references as possible and always hand sign them. Your effect on the reader will be greater.

Strive to be brief while still conveying the most important and relevant information. Your letter should emphasize the benefits to the reader. The timing is also important—don't mail when everyone else is mailing—choose a time when a new competitor enters your arena or when a particular season begins. Personal letters are relatively inexpensive. All you need is the time to write good ones, a quality printer, and the postage to send them.

On the next page, we have included a copy of a personal letter from a security business. The style of this letter could be of use to almost any service or professional.

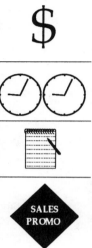

SALES
PROMO

Jones Security Service
1221 Safe Way
Security, CA 99999
(000) 222-SAFE

September 1, 1993

Dear Mr. Green:

Did you realize there are 10 burglaries every day in your community?

When you're away who's watching your home? Are your windows and doors burglar-proof? Do your neighbors keep an eye on your place? Have you looked into alarm systems, only to discover they cost a small fortune?

Good security means security that is cost-effective. And it means a service which uses employees with mature, level heads and a lot of experience in the security business.

That's what the Jones Security Service is all about. Round the clock protection for your home while you're away by mature, experienced personnel at reasonable prices.

Jones Security Service employs seniors who can remain in your home while you're away. Housesitters who have attended special seminars on home security. And since they're retired, they aren't spending eight hours a day in an office or trying to get out of town for the weekend. They're there to protect your home, and tend to your pets if necessary.

Enclosed is a brochure detailing our services. You'll also find all of our employees are bonded and have excellent references. And we can guarantee that our security service rates for weekends, weeks or months will be the lowest rates in town.

So when you're out of town, call us—it will be one less thing to worry about.

Sincerely,

John P. Jones
President

Personal Recommendations

see: Referral, Networking, Testimonials

Personal recommendations are also known as word-of-mouth. This form of attracting new business is the most powerful marketing tool you can have, as well as, being the most cost effective. Word-of-mouth referrals take time to develop, but when it catches on, you see your business grow geometrically.

When new business comes to you because of a referral, it comes to you at a lower cost than the client who saw an ad or picked up a brochure. Numerous studies show that referral business is both more likely to return and more apt to tell a friend about your business. Word-of-mouth works for all businesses, both products and services. Whenever possible, find out how people heard of your business—get the name of the referring person and personally acknowledge them. Knowing how you are getting business will also help you in planning future marketing programs.

Placards/Mass Transit Signs

see: billboards

The signs you see on transit vehicles, the buses, taxies, trains, subways, on the benches and at local stops are sometimes referred to placards. This medium, like billboards, is another way to generate visibility and name recognition. This medium is most often used by large, local businesses or by nationally-known companies.

If you are a small business in a large city, this medium probably won't do you a lot of good because it's hard to target, and the people you reach may not necessarily have access to what you are offering for a lot of reasons (for example, location). Like billboards, placards are designed to create an image and visibility, not necessarily to sell. If, however, your business is located in a small community and you can get your ads on the benches and at the bus stop near to your location, that may well help your business. It is important to note, however, that in a smaller community, those who use the transit system are often seniors, teens and those without cars. If these demographic groups are among your target audience, placards could be a very reasonable and cost-effective means of reaching them. Please note that in order to find what works, you may have to experiment—and that, in and of itself, could be expensive.

Press Conference

see: press release, media relations

A press conference, sometimes called a news conference, is a conference or meeting attended by the press for the purpose of making an important announcement. Holding a press conference does not usually work for feature stories, though, there may be some exceptions to this rule.

Press conferences take planning, but are often done on very short notice. You must make preparations, for example: where to hold it, make arrangements for key people to be present and have printed information such as press kits that support the announcement. Usually a considerable amount of money is needed by the time all the arrangements are finished.

Before you go and plan a news conference, ask yourself the following:

Is my announcement hard news? For example: is it a breakthrough in AIDS research, has a major company filed bankruptcy, or is it an announcement to run for a political office, etc.

Can I make a few phone calls to key media people and accomplish the same result? You can always follow up to the rest of the media with a press release.

If it is not hard news, will it be visual, or will you have many prominent names in one place for interviewing convenience? Often if you have several celebrities supporting a project you can get the media to attend.

What is the reason to have all the press there at one specific time? Timing is everything—you don't want to exclude any media because of deadlines.

Keep in mind, that even if you get a firm commitment from the press that they will attend, there's always the chance that a disaster, whether it's a fire, an earthquake, or a flood will occur and no one will show.

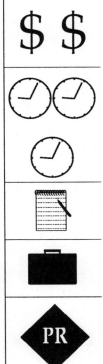

Often your best bet in planning a press conference is to hire the expertise of a public relations professional. She/he knows the best times, who will or won't attend, and can do the follow up to get the most mileage out of the event once it is over.

Press Kit

see: collateral materials

A press kit, some times called a media kit, contains all the information a media person needs to know about a business, product or person. A good press kit will have more information than can actually be used, but it's better to provide too much than too little. The key to gaining press attention is to make it as easy as possible for the reporter to create a news or feature story.

The cost of a press kit can vary dramatically, but it should not break your budget. The important point here is to take the time to make sure your press kit is professional looking, clearly written, grammatically correct and well organized. If necessary, consult a public relations professional for advice, or a desktop graphics person to help with the layout.

The elements of a press kit include the following:

1. Fact Sheet—A brief, one-page outline of the business/ product's description, purpose, location and hours of business, key people involved, and how and when it started. Some of these may not be appropriate for your kit, so use your judgment. A fact sheet is just that—the facts, this is not the place to include opinions.

2. A press release—the release can be about a grand opening, the introduction of a new product or new research findings. Again, it will depend on the nature of your business.

3. A biographical sketch of the owner(s), not necessarily a resume, but a history that runs about a half to a full page.

4. Photos when appropriate. If the press kit is designed to promote a professional, then a photo of her/him is in order. If it is a product, then a picture of it, or if it is a business, maybe a picture of the building showing the business.

5. Other items that can also be included in this package include copies of previous newspaper clippings, brochures, promotional items, and samples or coupons.

Press Release

see: press conference, publicity, public relations, media relations

Next to the telephone, the press release is the most important vehicle for disseminating information about an event, program, activity, or research results. When successfully done, the release becomes a news story in itself or leads to one. To ensure that your press release is read and used, it is essential that it be typed, clearly written and presented in the release format. Here are some guidelines to writing a press release.

1. Use the 8 1/2 x 11 letterhead stationery of your business or organization. If you don't have stationery, type your name, address and phone number in the upper left hand corner.

2. Use a headline to start off your release. It should be catchy, reveal what the story is about and not more than two lines.

3. The first paragraph, called the lead, is where you indicate the who, what, where and when. It's the most important—you need to grab the readers' attention so they will read on! The why and how follow in the second paragraph. The most newsworthy and basic information should be written in the first two paragraphs. The rest of the release is devoted to additional details, quotes, statistics and background material. Always use double spacing.

4. Releases should be written in journalistic style. Study the newspaper to get a feel for this type of writing. This means it should be objective, should not contain opinions, and must be accurate, brief and clearly written.

5. Be exact. Always give a date and time, the name and address of the location. Check names for correct spelling and spell out numbers one through nine, for numbers ten and above, use numerals.

6. If you receive coverage, write a thank you note to the paper or reporter to express appreciation.

On the upper right side of a press release are the date and beneath the date is the CONTACT, that is the person to be called if the reporter has additional questions or wants to set up a photo shoot. It is important that someone be at that number.

FOR IMMEDIATE RELEASE is all upper case on the left side— you'll want it to be considered immediately. Next comes the headline which tells the reporter the gist of the story.

Releases should not be more than two pages. If you need a second page, type the word "more" at the bottom. On the next page at the top, repeat the headline and write page 2, staple the two sheets together. At the end of your release, type ### to indicate The End.

Once the release is ready to go, you need to compile a media mailing list. You can find many of the names you want in the Yellow Pages, in a media registry published locally, or at the library. Be sure you have the proper name and spelling of the publication or station. It is also wise to call and ask for the name of the person to send it to, whether it is the city, medical, business or travel editor or reporter.

Not every media person in town should receive your release—it depends on the release's content, the type of story, and the area in which it is located. Use your judgment in selecting your targeted media. If you are not sure, call and ask. It will save you postage and time in follow up calls. On the following page is a sample release to give you a feel for what they should look like.

If your press release is tied to a specific event, holiday or timetable, you should find out the editorial deadlines for the publications of interest to you. Magazines work many months in advance. News-papers, particularly smaller local newspapers, often have shorter lead times. Nonetheless, they may have specific issues with corre-sponding deadlines.

If you are uncomfortable with the thought of writing a press release, your other option is a fact sheet. This is a one page sheet that gives the facts on your event—the who, what, when, where, and why. You'll find a sample fact sheet right after the press release.

If you have a major event with many components and/or many different story angles, it may well be necessary to have both a release and a fact sheet. The fact sheet gives just the facts of the event, and the press releases are written to focus on specific story angles, such as business or health.

FOR IMMEDIATE RELEASE
Students get Skinned at Anytown High School on May 10

Before summer vacation begins, students at Anytown High School will be skinned....that is evaluated for early warning signs of skin cancer by the Skinmobil, a mobile unit provided by the local dermatology group. The group sponsoring the screening on May 10, at 10 a.m. is the XYZ auxiliary of the cancer association. The school is located at 555 Main St.

The skinmobil, armed with six dermatologists and their staffs will give students a 20-minute evaluation to check for early signs of skin cancer such as itchy, dry flaky skin, sores that don't heal and suspicious looking moles. The areas that concern physicians the most are the face, specifically the nose, arms, and the neck.

"Our goal is to make students aware of the problem now because in 10 years it will be too late," said Jane Doe, spokeswoman for XYZ auxiliary. "The teen years are when the sun's ultraviolet rays do the most damage to the skin."

While this is the first time teens are the target for this screening, it will be an annual event, said Doe.

Following the evaluation, students will receive samples of sun block with SPF 15 or higher—just in time for the sun and fun that usually comes with summer vacations.

Anytown High School is the first school in this city to host such an event. Doe said she hopes other schools will also implement such a program.

###

Date
CONTACT: Name
Phone number

FACT SHEET

FOR IMMEDIATE RELEASE
Students get skinned at Anytown High School

WHO: Students at Anytown High School will be skinned, that is screened for early warning signs of skin cancer on the school's campus. The group sponsoring the screening is the XYZ auxiliary of the cancer association.

WHAT: The XYZ auxiliary has arranged for the cancer association's Skinmobil, a mobile unit staffed by local dermatologists to conduct the screenings. The doctors will provide students with a 20 minute evaluation to check for early signs of skin cancer such as itchy, dry flaky skin, sores that don't heal and suspicious looking moles. The areas that concern physicians the most are the face, specifically the nose, arms, and the neck.

WHERE: The school is located at 555 Main St. Anytown, phone number.

WHEN : May 10, at 10 a.m.

WHY: The teen years are when the sun's ultraviolet rays do the most damage to the skin. The goal is to make students aware of the problem now because in 10 years it will be too late. This is the first time teens are the target for this screening, and it will be an annual event. Following the evaluation, students will receive samples of sun block with SPF 15 or higher—just in time for the sun and fun that usually comes with summer vacations. Anytown High School is the first school in this city for such an event.

###

Publicity

see: grand openings, media relations, public relations, press releases, PSAs, writing for publications

Publicity is a special part of the larger public relations function. It specifically involves securing placement of information in the editorial sections of the media, not the advertising areas. Publicity includes such specific events as an appearance on a radio or TV talk show, an interview with a reporter, a feature story in a newspaper or magazine, or a reference to your activities in a journal. Publicity is the kind of advertisement that all the money in the world cannot buy. Most people realize this, and that is why this type of exposure usually carries a greater impact.

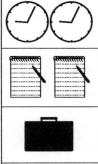

Favorable publicity gives a service/product a great deal of visibility for attracting new business, while reinforcing its image among existing businesses.

The key to gaining publicity is to have a story of interest, a news hook. Your publicity, like other marketing efforts must be targeted to an identifiable segment of the public. Knowing what media your prospective customers read or watch also determines where you will try to gain publicity. Most of the time you will have to approach the media yourself (usually through press releases) and make yourself available to them. You can also contact local newspaper editors about writing a feature article or responding in the "Letters to the Editor" section.

To book an appearance on TV or radio talk shows, first decide which ones are most appropriate, find out the producers' name, send them a press release and a photo if and when appropriate. Always follow up with a phone call. Any interesting visual aspects of your business that you can exploit will increase your chances of an appearance. If you are asked to appear, provide a press kit, or at least a one-page biographical sketch of yourself and your business to ensure the host has enough background to make the interview interesting and memorable. You may even want to provide the host with a sheet of questions to which you have prepared interesting answers.

As a whole, publicity provides an inexpensive way to bolster your image and visibility among thousands of potential customers and it presents you as an expert in your field. Because your story is presented as news, and not paid-for advertising, it implies the endorsement of that medium. However, there is a downside. You do not have any control of the outcome of your publicity efforts. It takes a lot of time, commitment to developing media contacts and creativity to find a story angle that appeals to a particular group. It also requires good PR skills and taking risks to gain rewards. Often you are wise to hire a professional publicist or PR agency to help out in this area.

Public Service Announcements (PSA's)

see: media relations, community involvement, charity events

Public service announcements are designed to promote an event or service that will benefit the welfare of the public at large or that operates in the public interest. Many organizations, commercial and non-commercial have utilized public service campaigns.

All types of mass media donate space and time to worthy causes for PSA's, but probably the easiest to get is free radio air time and newspaper listings.

If you are doing something of community interest in your business, then you may be eligible. While some radio stations say they limit PSA's to nonprofit groups, this rule is loosely enforced and they will accept PSAs from a profit organization if it truly benefits the community. You will have a better chance of qualifying for free coverage if a large portion of the event's proceeds benefit a charity.

Here are some tips on getting PSA coverage for your event.

1. Plan ahead and send your PSA to the stations four to six weeks prior to the event.

2. Select appropriate stations for the event. Each station has a personality with specific demographics. (If your event is targeted to seniors, the local rock station is probably not an appropriate market.)

3. PSAs have to be short, so keep your sentences simple and snappy. Most stations use 10- or 30-second spots. Call and find out which they prefer. The less work you make for them, the better are your chances of getting aired.

4. After sending or delivering your copy to the PSA director, (use a name whenever possible), follow up with a call.

5. Be accommodating to the station. They do not make money, and if you are cooperative they will be too.

On the following page is an example of a PSA format. Along with the PSA you should also include a press release and a fact sheet if available. Each PSA should be submitted on a separate sheet of paper, double-spaced with the date, a contact person the station can call with questions, the PSA air dates and a brief title.

Date
Contact: Name
Phone number

Air Dates—Mar.1-7
<u>*Get Screened at the Free Health Fair*</u>
:10 PSA

IT'S NATIONAL HEALTH WEEK...GET SCREENED FROM HEAD TO TOE AT THE FREE HEALTH FAIR EXPO ON SATURDAY, MARCH 7, FROM 10 TO 2 AT ABC MEDICAL CLINIC IN YOUR TOWN. FOR INFORMATION CALL THIS STATION.

###

Date
Contact: Name
Phone number

Air Dates—Mar.1-7
<u>*Get Screened at the Free Health Fair*</u>
:30 PSA

BE A PART OF NATIONAL HEALTH WEEK ... GET SCREENED FROM HEAD TO TOE AT THE FREE HEALTH FAIR EXPO ON SATURDAY, MARCH 7, FROM 10 TO 2 AT ABC MEDICAL CLINIC, IN YOUR TOWN. THERE'LL BE SCREENING FOR VISION, CHOLESTEROL LEVELS, SKIN CANCER, BODY FAT, BLOOD PRESSURE AND POSTURE ANALYSIS. ALSO ENJOY A FREE MINI HEAD AND NECK MASSAGE AND EVALU-ATE YOUR EATING HABITS. THEN WATCH DEMONSTRATIONS ON AEROBIC EXERCISE, YOGA AND TAI CHI AND TAKE HOME A HEALTH KIT LOADED WITH PRODUCT SAMPLES AND COUPONS. FOR MORE INFORMATION CALL THIS STATION.

###

Public Relations

see: media relations, press conference, press release, PSA, publicity

Public relations (PR) efforts should be an important part of your marketing plan. No matter how you look at it, public relations and advertising go hand in hand...each reinforcing the other to make a stronger marketing program.

In a broad sense, public relations means communications activities that have not been paid for directly and that inform various markets about yourself, your business or your products. Public relations usually means free publicity that results from news articles about you or your business. But it also includes corporate and institutional advertising, recruitment advertising, lobbying, sponsorship of special events, fund-raising efforts, posters, exhibits, videocassettes and more.

The positive aspects of PR are that it adds credibility and authority, builds a strong identity and is often free.

On the negative side—you don't have control over what is aired or printed, when it runs, how it is presented, or its accuracy. It is also rarely repeated, and you cannot buy it, though advertorial advertising sometimes come close.

If your business is unusual and offers a lot of PR possibilities, you may be wise in consulting a PR professional.

In order to be successful at your own public relations campaign, you will need three things:

1. imagination to generate legitimate news that is worth publicizing;
2. media contacts to get your news story published;
3. time and persistence to follow through.

To generate PR, you will need to create newsworthy events out of your normal activities. If you are active in environmental research, establish a relationship with the science and/or environmental writers. If you give a speech on a specific topic, offer a seminar, or present a special guest, send out a press release to receive press coverage. If you have a big newsworthy announcement to make, consider holding a press conference. But to get the media to attend, it must be legitimate news or it must be very visual. In most cases, You are best off in hiring a PR professional to handle a news conference (see press conference).

When contacting the media for any reason, whether it be a seminar, new research findings, or a free demonstration, your news or announcement must be submitted in a written form called a press release (see press releases) to a specific department or person.

Public Speaking

see: conferences, seminars, workshops, networking through associations

Public speaking is an excellent public relations tools for building an individual's reputation and name recognition for a business with a product or service to sell. Groups of all kinds seek speakers to address their members, and it's a good way to educate people about your field without promoting your business directly.

To get headed in this direction make a list of topics about which you could be speaking. Get a little bit more depth, develop an interesting title and maybe even a speech outline. Then to schedule engagements, contact those groups whose members are good potential business. If you are selling maternity clothing, choose various women's groups or even pregnant women's classes. Make a list of groups that could be interested in your topic.

You might also want to register with a speakers' bureau or other organization; however, be aware that most speakers groups want a list of groups they can call for a reference. This is especially true in cases where a fee/honorarium may be paid.

Most small business owners who speak publicly are non-writers, meaning that we don't write for a living, so writing your speech will no doubt be one of the most dreaded and procrastinated activities. As your thoughts are placed on the paper, every word will be pondered, sweated and analyzed, only to discover when you're done that it sounds dull, stiff and unorganized.

The following are a few suggestions to avoid some of the most common mistakes when writing and presenting a speech. When you are actually writing your copy, organize your speech into three parts.

1. What you are going to talk about/present, or what you want to accomplish.

2. Next is the actual information, the meat of your topic, how you accomplish what it is that you do.

3. Then a summation or a reiteration of what you've presented or the accomplishments.

Very simply stated, you tell them what you are going to tell them, tell them, and then tell them what you've told them.

Be conversational, use everyday language with contractions and don't be afraid to use a local or regional dialect style as long as it is one shared by your audience. It can only help in your communication to them. Also be sure to use gestures, it is an added form of communication. Then speak, speak and speak again! Start with smaller groups and work your way up.

When you are giving your speech/presentation, also consider if it would help to use visual aids. Providing visuals can help to reinforce a point, make an abstract concept clearer, offer proof of what you are talking about and/or give the audience a focal point. It also helps to take some of the focus off you, as well as to take your mind off of your stage fright.

Visual aids don't have to be expensive. They can be as simple as:

- A blackboard, though this can sometimes be perceived as a school teacher approach

- Magnetic boards & easels

- Building Blocks. You can use the giant-sized children's toys and place words or sentences on one side and stack them to communicate a message.

- Flash cards

- Before & after samples

The most crucial factor in using visual aids well is knowing your material and having the confidence to stand and deliver.

Rehearse out loud, even record yourself with a tape recorder or video camera. By doing this, the dull parts and the unclear material will jump out. Rework it, and try again! You may even want to enroll in a group such as Toastmasters International whose weekly meetings are focused on supporting members to be better public speakers.

Radio

see: advertising

Over the years research has proven that information that comes by sound is more easily remembered than information attained visually.

Since radio is considered the most personal way to advertise, commercials should have an emotional touch and should be direct. Radio is also the only medium that can be heard almost anywhere at any time and is considered a personal medium. Radio stations also have a more defined demographic audience than television. Just about all small businesses can benefit from this type of advertising. Creating an ad for radio is all about creatively used words, sounds, music and often humor. Together they must paint a visual image or feeling that persuades the listener to buy what your business is offering.

One of the important things about a radio commercial is that it fit with the format of the station on which it will be aired. That includes the words, style and music. If your ad is airing on a country western station, it is not appropriate to have an ad using hip lingo and rock music background. You want the listening audience to be able to relate to your message, so tailor the copy to those listeners! Listen to the station, before you create an ad.

When you are developing an ad, you have two options. Often the station will write and produce an ad as part of the cost of advertising. However, if you go this route, be sure to work with the copywriters so that the right message comes across. It is best to emphasize one point at a time. If you have many points that must be covered, be sure they have a central theme such as bargains, luxury or unique. Remember, you only have 30 or 60 seconds to get your message across, so keep it simple and to the point.

The other option in producing a commercial or a series of ads, is to hire a production company. In most cases, you will have a commercial that is of a better quality, is more creative and is more likely to stand out. But in order to do this, you will need to have already established the station(s) that work best for your product/service and then have the ad(s) geared to those listeners. Once it is well produced you can use it over and over again.

With radio, frequency is very important. When buying an advertising schedule, be sure your message gets a good rotation—that it is heard at many different times throughout the day or week. Your sales representative, will help you with placement and frequency. The cost to buy 60 seconds of time will vary depending on the times you buy, the market you are in and the strength of the station. If your budget is slim, you can stretch your dollars by mixing expensive times with less-expensive times. The most costly times to buy are morning and afternoon drive times.

Referral Development

see: networking, associations, personal recommendation

As we have mentioned throughout this book, personal referrals are an excellent way to generate new business. When new business is recommended to you by a competitor or an associate, then a personal reference has occurred. There are three methods that most small businesses use to secure referrals.

1. Encourage or request referrals in writing or verbally from present customers and clients

2. Become a part of a referral development network with other business people

3. Solicit referrals from other professionals who are either too busy to handle new clients or don't specialized in your area.

For referrals that turn into paying customers, consider offering a reward or finder's fee to encourage people to refer to you again. Since the referral has saved you the expense and time connected with attracting new business through ads, the fee is justified. Besides offering a reward, be sure to acknowledge your appreciation and follow up with both the potential client and the party who made the referral. A thank you not is always appreciated. Little promotional expense is required, but it takes time to build a solid referral network. And of course, your existing clients must be satisfied with your product or service in order to perpetuate referrals.

Refunds/Guarantees

see: customer relations, sales promotion

"Satisfaction guaranteed or your money back" is a common enough phrase, but its results are anything but common. "Guaranteed or your money refunded" is an essential part of a small business and can make or break a sale. Guarantees are a great tool to encourage sales of unknown products or new services. What better way to get people to buy and try your items than to guarantee they will like it.

Think of how many times you thought about making a purchase but weren't sure if you'd like it, or you weren't sure of how it would fit or whatever. Did knowing that you could return it for a refund make you more likely to buy it? Now think about this, how many times was the merchandise actually returned? A guarantee alllows the potential buyer to risk the purchase. If nothing else, a guarantee or refund policy builds goodwill for future purchases.

Businesses that deal with mail orders, where products and services are purchased unseen, are almost required to offer some sort of guaranteed satisfaction. These guarantees may take several forms. It can mean a full cash refund when returning a product, full store credit on product exchanges, or a cash discount on future purchases. If your service or product is seasonal, you might consider an extended time guarantee to encourage off-season sales, and boost year around business. Some offers even allow for a trial use basis.

Another way of reinforcing your guarantee is to use a third party endorsement. An example of this would be "The Good Housekeeping Seal of Approval" or some other organization endorsement such as a Physicians' approval for a health or child safety product. Again, if your company uses direct mail, you will probably need some form of satisfaction guarantee.

Sales Awards & Incentives

see: customer relations, customer appreciation programs, in store displays

A sales award or incentive may mean something different to each business owner who ponders the concept. But all will agree the goal of these programs is to increase sales or to create a more efficient business operation.

Sales awards/incentives are used as an internal marketing tool to motivate a sales staff to produce a wanted results whether it is increase sales, increase customer satisfaction, or help the business run more smoothly. Awards can also be used to create employee pride with programs like "employee of the month" or "salesperson of the quarter." Awards don't necessarily have to involve monetary compensation. They can be a certificate or plaque of appreciation, a special parking space or a simple employee party given in his/her honor.

Sales incentives (as opposed to awards) generally involve some kind of financial gain for a job well done. When incentives take the form of a sales commission, they are usually paid on a monthly, quarterly, or yearly basis, depending on the type of business. A sales commission can also be the primary method by which an employee earns his/her money or it can be in addition to an hourly or salary wage. Regardless of what program you choose to use, the incentive schedule should be clearly spelled out so that there is no confusion. When a business offers an award or incentive program, it is very important to set an evaluation criteria with measurable standards by which an employee's performance can be judged. These standards must be clearly stated and easily understood.

Sales Promotion

see: advertising, coupons, demonstrations, grand openings, in store displays, public relations, trade shows

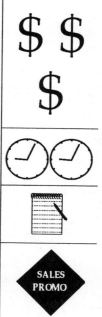

A promotion is an action designed to get a response to a message whether it comes in the form of an advertisement, a discount coupon, a point of purchase display (POP) or a special demonstration. Each will give you a different response. But in all cases, the best sales promotions are those that get their point across quickly and simply. Promotions work best when they are tied-in with advertising, public relations and other sales programs and should only in rare cases be used by themselves.

Sales promotion is an additional way to supplement advertising campaigns and personal selling. It may be used to generate sales leads, get people to try a new service or product, (for example, offer free demonstration or sample, or discount coupon), or to get additional retail space for a special promotion. It can also take the form of a grand opening in which more than one of these tactics can be used.

Different sales promotion tools will generate a different response. For example, couponing can increase trial of your product (among people who don't currently use your product), increase sales to people who already use your product, or can push light, infrequent users to purchase in greater quantities. If you are a retail business, coupons can have similar kinds of effects on usage of your store or restaurant.

Giveaways or premiums can help customers try your product at no risk. The results could be life-long customers. Displays can help you obtain more attention for a specific product or event. Demonstrations can help you show potential customers the advantages of your product. In each case, the promotional tool used should address the marketing problem you are trying to solve.

Therefore, the first step, before deciding to coupon, or spend money on an expensive display or premium-size, is to decide what you want to accomplish. Maybe you want to:

- increase the frequency with which people visit your restaurant, or

- you have a terrific dinner business and you'd like to get people to come in for lunch, or

- people aren't very aware of your product and you'd like to get them to try it, or

- you have terrific seasonal usage (for example, Christmas or tax season) and you would like to obtain usage at other times of the year.

Each of these problems can be tackled, at least in part, by a good sales promotion program. Start by defining your objective, then sit with some friends and make a list of the kinds of programs that might work. Take a look at what your competitors are doing. You don't need to copy them, but it can start your creative juices flowing. Talk to your vendors and your customers. Look at the local paper. Put together a list of potential sales promotion programs to tackle what you see as the big issue.

When setting up a sales promotion, decide exactly what is to be accomplished. That means you need to determine your market; who the promotion is designed to attract; set goals that can be measured, either by increased traffic or inquiries; and, then designate a time frame within which to measure response.

When designing a promotional offer, set it up on a limited basis either by area or time. If it is on-going, it is not a promotion and you stand to lose money, and product value over the long-term.

Seminars

see: conferences, education, public speaking, workshops

Seminars are a popular and effective way to educate your market as to what your business offers, whether it's a service or product. They can last an hour or a full day, and the tuition can vary from being free to hundreds of dollars. Seminars are educational in nature and can provide information alone, or information plus hands-on training. They can also be used as a marketing tool to attract new business, or generate profit from your existing business. Seminars are particularly recommended if you're looking for new business or offering new services, especially if what you are doing is innovative. The advantages to seminars are numerous. They:

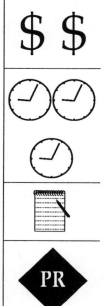

- enable you to meet prospective clients face-to-face

- provide the opportunity for you to demonstrate your specialty skills to an audience before they have to make a commitment

- allow you to reach many people at one time

- enhance your professional authority, reputation, and credibility

- can be easily repeated once the initial presentation and materials have been developed; and

- when combined with advertising and PR, they create visibility for your business, regardless of the attendance.

Finding a location to have your seminar can present you with many choices. If your office is large enough and appropriate, you can have the event there or in your building's conference room. There are many companies in the business of renting meeting room space and that is often less expensive than hotel space. Use of hotel meeting rooms can be costly, but if your seminar warrants the expense, you will be provided with many services along with the prestige of a well-known location.

The general rule regarding refreshments depends on the length of your seminar. For an hour or less, you don't need to provide anything. For a three to four hour event, providing water, coffee and tea (doughnuts if it's a morning time frame) is recommended. A full-day's event might include morning refreshments and, at a minimum, a boxed lunch. Or add the lunch cost to the seminar fee and have a congenial sit-down meal so that participants can interact with you and each other.

Remember that a poor seminar can damage your reputation. Probably the best way to get into seminar production is to start with a short, free event so that you can get used to the routine and ensure everything works smoothly. One way to begin is by offering "brown bag" events during the lunch hour or short after-work seminars at your office. Both of these will allow you to test various subjects without incurring a high cost.

There are some drawbacks to holding seminars. Significant time and effort are required to prepare a good program. It can be expensive to promote your event through ads, direct mail, brochures and other means of communication. This can be a high risk endeavor if your fixed expenses are high. There is always uncertainty about whether the participation level will cover expenses and generate a profit or if the content will attract interest and adequate participation. Finally, you must not only be able to educate the audience but you must also be able to sell to them— that is, have them want to seek your business out after the seminar and possibly refer new business.

Sponsored Courses

see: educational programs, seminars, workshops

If you are more than a terrific speaker and have the talent to instruct others in a classroom setting, consider teaching a sponsored course. Numerous organizations offer courses for credit and non-credit in a variety of subject matter.

Courses may range from a one day session, to a series of evenings or even a semester. As an instructor you are usually paid a stipend. More importantly, your name will be listed in the class schedule and widely distributed throughout the community.

The sponsoring groups are usually colleges, universities, community colleges professional and educational associations, libraries, and other public education forums. They are responsible for all promotional efforts so there is no financial risk to you.

Teaching a class allows you to personally illustrate your expertise to potential clients and referral sources, which in turn contributes to the reputation and credibility of your business/practice. Course materials also make excellent tools to reuse later for seminars, speeches, etc. Your cost is limited to the time it takes to create the materials, and develop and deliver the lectures.

Telemarketing

see: direct mail, sales

Telemarketing involves telephoning potential customers or referral sources to generate interest in your services. Often the aim is to get a chance to meet with them to determine how you can be of assistance to them. This is referred to as outbound telemarketing. Inbound telemarketing is when you have trained personnel ready to respond to a variety of sales promotion activities. These phone calls often come in on 800 numbers. Callers are often cross marketed to close a sale.

The major benefit of telemarketing is its efficiency as a means of reaching large numbers of potential clients on a personal level. Costs will vary. If you do the calling yourself and use your own lists, then your costs are only your time and the calls themselves. But if you need to hire a telemarketing person or firm, and have to buy specialized lists, then you will incur increased expenses. Either way excellent telephone skills are needed to prevent sounding like a broken record.

For the best results, you should make an initial offering at no cost and no obligation to the prospect. Some pointers on preparing a sales call are:

- create an outline to collect your ideas and prepare a script

- make sure your speech does not sound like an ad

- include questions to your prospect and places for them to respond

- don't memorize your script, but use it to keep yourself on track and

- be sure your script can handle several situations.

When you place the actual call, be brief and to the point, friendly, emphasize benefits and close clearly.

Often a telemarketing call will serve as a follow up to a direct mail piece or some other promotional material. The impersonal mail piece paves the way for the personal telephone call and increases the response rate of the mailing. Another method is to call first, to qualify interest in your product/service, and then send information to interested prospects.

Telemarketing can be done on an ongoing basis or on an as needed basis, depending on your desire for new business. Telemarketing is an effective method of building business and it allows you to quickly assess their need or interest in your business. However, not every business is an appropriate one to telemarket—use your judgment.

Television

see: cable television

These days nearly 100% of the homes have a television set in them. TV is a mass medium in the truest form, reaching the most people at any one time. That's also why it can be so expensive to use as a medium for advertising.

All businesses would love to see their ads on TV, and just by running TV spots a business can gain prestige. That's because most people have a vague idea of the cost of TV ads, so just by being seen, people assume the business is doing well. But unfortunately, TV advertising is usually too expensive for the small business owner. It is not just the cost of buying air time, but the cost of producing the ads.

If your budget allows for TV ads and it fits with your marketing plan, you'll gain many benefits. TV reaches audiences locally, regionally or nationally depending on the type of programming. That is particularly good for businesses with multiple locations or products with national distribution. If you choose to place ads in specific time frames or during specific shows, you are reasonably assured the same viewers are watching, giving your ads consistent viewing. You can target your market by the programs in which you advertise. TV is also a medium that appeals to both sight and sound, and is ideal for demonstrations of products/services. But it is very expensive, the remote control makes it easy to switch channels and the best shows also cost the most money.

Several things to consider before including television ads in your marketing plan would be:

- *Is the product/service geared for a sight and sound ad?* Can you easily demonstrate how the product works, or is it visual.

- *Is your area of trade wide or narrow?* TV is a mass medium, your product/service should appeal to the average consumer.

- *Can you afford the cost of producing an ad?*

- *Will the ad budget allow you to buy enough air time to get a well-rounded schedule?*

The answers to these questions will basically tell you if television is the medium for you.

However, if you really want your ads to run on television you might also consider a few alternatives such as cable programming and non-network stations. Non-network (more local) stations are beginning to hold their own in terms of audience and have less expensive advertising space.

You might also use cable, local and non-premium network to test a campaign in before developing an expensive TV ad campaign.

Testimonials

see: display advertising, TV & cable

Building an advertising and public relations campaign around testimonials is nothing new...it's done all the time and it works! What better way to give credibility to a new business than via already satisfied customers/clients or a celebrity. You'll also find that some of your best selling phrases may come from those who know the product or service.

Testimonials are used in all forms of advertising, from direct mail to print and electronic ads. An example of a testimonial print ad is when you see a critic's quotes about how great a movie is or how riveting a book was to read. Television also makes great use of testimonial ads—vocational schools have used former students and attorneys have relied on satisfied clients. When you think about it, a person who has had a positive experience with a product or service can be very convincing. Many companies when looking for new sales staff, hire former customers who know the business and believe in what they are selling.

If you use testimonials in your advertising be sure to get the okay of the testimonial donor. That usually means signing a simple release form that says something to the effect of, "you have my permission to use..." If you have any questions, consult with your attorney—just in case. Most people are more than happy to lend their quotes.

The other type of testimonial, uses a celebrity, either local or national, to sell a product or service. If you use a recognizable person, make sure it makes sense for that person to represent your business. If you have a comedy club, an appropriate person might be a well-know radio DJ or a local comedian who's made the big time. But keep in mind, how that person conducts him/herself and is perceived by the public can be a reflection on your business....both in good and bad times.

Toll-Free Numbers

see: telemarketing, sales

Americans order millions of dollars in goods over the telephone every day and though you may not be selling catalog items, establishing a toll-free phone number is still an effective way to greatly increase the response rate of your promotional efforts.

"800" numbers are most commonly used in conjunction with direct mail offers, but once your number is established, use it on all your materials such as stationery, brochures, specialty items, etc. as a benefit to customers. An "800" number can enhance the marketing power of your promotional materials. You could also establish it as a "hotline" for answering questions.

There are different types of toll-free numbers. Your local phone company can discuss costs and options. However, if you go through the expense of establishing an 800 number, make sure you have a staff person ready to answer the calls.

$

SALES
PROMO

Trade Shows

see: Education, Fairs, Conferences

More than 9,000 trade shows are held in the U.S. yearly and cover every industry from leisure, to electronics, to gourmet food and beyond. Displaying goods and services at trade shows, exhibits and fairs is sometimes the only method of marketing used by some businesses. They put all their effort and money into exhibiting and selling their merchandise at trade shows because they know many serious prospects will attend these events. Trade shows are usually geared to selling products rather than services. They are most often designed for wholesalers and retailers, and are not usually aimed at the average consumer.

For the small business owner, renting a booth and trying to market your business at a national or even regional show can be a difficult task and expensive. In some instances, you would be wise to find a local trade show that is on a smaller scale and attracts predominately the local market. Additionally, professional organizations often hold exhibits for special events. Having a simple but professional-looking booth or display at one of these shows can be very beneficial in making new contacts and increasing visibility. Keep in mind if you are a new business, your booth at the trade show will be the first impression to many, so be sure it looks professional. Also remember, you do not always need to buy an exhibit, there are companies that rent exhibit booths and customize them to fit your needs at a fraction of the cost.

In determining if a trade show will benefit your business—ask yourself the following questions:

1. How many people/prospects will you reach and what type of people are they?

2. How much do you have to invest to get to these people?

3. Is the cost per person worth it?

4. Is there a better way to reach your targeted market?

5. What type of exhibit will you need?

6. What type of show is it—a large show with general appeal or a very targeted show?

7. Is it a new show or one that has a track record for success?

If your goals are to build an image, your money may be better spent on advertising and public relations. If your goal is to make sales and gain sales leads, could you better reach your market through direct mail?

If this tool is for you, be sure the assistants attending the booth are friendly and educated about your business, that they stay close to the booth, that they make eye contact with those they talk to and try not to offend others by smoking, chewing gum, or eating. Always create a positive impression, by dressing professionally and wearing a badge with your name clearly visible. And take the responsibility for engaging in conversation and finding out what the visitor needs. While some of these may be obvious pointers to you, make sure your staff is also aware of them, you'd be surprised how many of these things you'll find happening as you walk around the show.

If trade shows are for you, be sure to have plenty of promotional, educational and selling materials to hand out to people who stop by your booth. That way they will see and remember your name or business when the show is over. Often it is a good idea to offer a drawing where people can sign up to enter, thus adding names to your database. You can also give away or sell advertising specialties with your name and logo.

The sponsor of the event usually publishes literature or a directory of participants. This is a great place to heighten name recognition. Since your main goal is to attract new business, have a system on hand so you can make future appointments if applicable.

Workshops

see: seminars, educational programs, sponsored courses, speeches

Workshops are described as a series of meetings for intensive study or discussion. Holding workshops for clients and prospective business can be an excellent way to educate. The benefits to you and your business-building efforts are the same as those for seminars. However, more time, effort and money must go into preparing and conducting a workshop.

Workshops usually concentrate on a specific area in a field and then focus on selective topics within that one area. Often there are several speakers on hand presenting the different topics. For example, if you have a hardware store, you could hold a workshop series for people remodeling homes. In your series you could present experts demonstrating how to re-tile, how to wall-paper a room, or how to install windows. This might attract those already loyal customers who are considering remodeling their home or are in the process of doing so, as well as, potential new business.

Yellow Pages

see: Directories, Display Ads

Here we look specifically at Yellow Pages directories. Directories in general are covered under "directories." Like directories, people looking in the Yellow Pages are ready to buy and looking for a place to buy it. Your ad must convince them to call your business first.

A few years ago, *Forbes* magazine identified Yellow Pages directories as the fastest-growing major advertising medium in the country. This type of promotion offers 24-hour availability and a long life expectancy.

The first thing you need to decide as a marketer is whether or not your business is the kind that can benefit from the Yellow Pages. Would most people look there to find a service or product like yours? Some of you may have immediately answered "no," while others answered "yes' or "maybe." Only you know your business and its clients. But in nearly all cases, a small business will benefit from being listed in the Yellow Pages. It may be helpful to consult current or old directories to see what others in your industry or field are doing or have done. If many in similar businesses or professions are listed, it's probably wise to give it a try.

Once you've decided to use this form, you'll need to determine which directories to be in—will one be sufficient, or will you have to be in five or more in a large city or country? Keep in mind that most businesses draw from their immediate area.

If you think you must run Yellow Pages ads in more than one directory, you then need to decide if those ads should be as big as your primary area ad, or smaller. There are many choices and possible combinations for Yellow Pages ads. They can be simple listings or elaborate ads in dark or regular type, color, or black and white. You also need to select the most appropriate category in which to place your ad.

Ads are usually billed monthly and are not cheap. When writing your ad, remember you are trying to attract new clients, so use the space to sell your expertise on a one-on-one basis. Other helpful tips:

- give people the facts and try to make it personal;

- emphasize your specialties by describing services that distinguish you from other competitors.

- Include as much information about your hours, availability, payment options, and directions to your location.

- If you offer free estimates or initial consultations include it in your ad.

- Make your ad look distinctive—use graphics if possible.

- Lastly, be aware of what your competition is doing, not necessarily to copy them, but to have a general idea of what's being done in your area.

A sample of a one inch directory listing is shown below. On the next page is an example of a much larger display ad.

SMITH ASSOCIATES ARCHITECTS & PLANNER
20 Business Park Drive
San Diego ......
(000) 000-0000

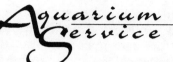

Specializing in

Salt Water
&
Fresh Water Tanks

- Installations

- Maintenance

FISH, ACCESSORIES & SUPPLIES

20 Mackerel Dr.
San Diego, CA 99999

For an immediate answer to
all your aquarium needs.

Dial: 1-800-4 FISHES

MACKEREL DRIVE

MAIN STREET

Yellow Pages display ad

900 Numbers

see: Directories, Yellow Pages, 800 numbers

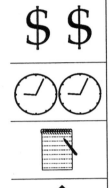

900 numbers are a new way of marketing a business and in some cases are the business itself. 900 numbers are a real advantage to businesses who offer referral information or services for which people are willing to pay. If you are interested in a 900 number, call your phone company for a brochure package on the specifics. But basically a business pays an installation fee and then can charge the caller anywhere from $2-5 for the first minute and $1-4 for each minute thereafter. The phone company charges approximately .25 cents for each minute used, and the rest goes to your business.

SOURCEBOOKS TRADE—
How-To Books For Today's Consumers

The Basics of Finance: Financial Tools for Non-Financial Managers
by Bryan E. Milling

Written in readable language, *The Basics of Finance* offers tools to help non-financial managers master financial information including understanding annual reports, interacting with financial personnel and using financial analysis to better understand the business world. An essential desk companion for any manager with direct or indirect financial responsibility ... and a key tool for professionals aspiring to the corner office.

210 pages ISBN 0-942061-18-7 (paperback) $14.95
ISBN 0-942061-25-X (hardcover) $24.95

Cash Flow Problem Solver: Common Problems and Practical Solutions
by Bryan E. Milling

Now in its third edition, *Cash Flow Problem Solver* is a proven bestseller and has helped over 20,000 business owners improve their cash flow and benefit from effective cash flow management. *Cash Flow Problem Solver* provides a results-oriented, step-by-step guide with tools and specific tactics to assure positive cash flow and to help boost a firm's profits. Cited as one of the three books on the "Smart CEO's Reading List" in INC Magazine. Selected as an alternate of both the **Business Week Book Club** and the **Fortune Book Club.**

296 pages ISBN 0-942061-27-6 (paperback) $19.95
0-942061-28-4 (hardcover) $32.95

Creating Your Own Future: A Woman's Guide to Retirement Planning
by Judith A. Martindale, CFP and Mary J. Moses

The authors argue that although retirement planning is important to everyone, factors unique to women, such as, shorter work lives due to child rearing, longer life expectancy, differing health needs than men, among others, make appropriate preparations essential.
 "Highly recommended" *Booklist*

256 pages ISBN 0-942061-09-8 (paperback) $14.95
0-942061-08-X (hardcover) $28.95

The Lifestyle Odyssey: The Facts Behind the Social, Personal and Cultural Changes Touching Each of Our Lives
by Eric Miller and the Editors of Research Alert

The Lifestyle Odyssey touches all social and cultural changes affecting our American lifestyle it takes us on a journey — a pathway describing a new American lifestyle. "The great changes of our lives come not with sound and fury but on the wings of doves." *Preface*
   " If you have but one life to live, read this book." says John Mack Carter, editor-in-chief of *Good Housekeeping* Magazine.

304 pages ISBN 0-942061-36-5 (paperback) $15.95
0-942061-31-4 (hardcover) $32.95

Future Vision: The 189 Most Important Trends of the 1990s
From the Editors of Research Alert

Our best-selling *Future Vision* gives substance to the dynamically changing forces that are reshaping America. Its unique presentation of both the facts and the fictions presents readers with an evenhanded perspective of what will happen next. . . with enough detail for them to see the implications of their own work.

256 pages ISBN 0-942061-16-0 (paperback) $12.95
0-942061-17-9 (hardcover) $21.95

Finding Time: Breathing Space For Women Who Do Too Much

by Paula Peisner

Finding Time: Breathing Space For Women Who Do Too Much shows women how to identify and eliminate actions by themselves and others that rob them of their most precious asset... time. This book is for all women who want to take control of thir own time and make more of it.

256 pages   ISBN 0-942061-33-0 (paperback) $7.95

Outsmarting the Competition: Practical Approaches to Finding and Using Competitive Information

by John J. McGonagle Jr. and Carolyn M. Vella

Competitive intelligence can give you some advance warning of the stirrings in your competitor's offices —without doing anything illegal or unethical. The first book to show what information you need and how to get it.

388 pages   IISBN 0-942061-04-7 (paperback) $17.95

The Small Business Survival Guide: How To Manage Your Cash, Profits and Taxes

by Robert E. Fleury

The Small Business Survival Guide includes discussions on: • planning for and filing taxes • cash flow analysis and management • understanding and developing financial statements • methods of taking and valuing inventory • how to value a business for buying and selling • managing your payroll & recordkeeping • PLUS...**NO-ENTRY ACCOUNTING...a means of doing and understanding your own accounting, without double-entry bookkeeping.**

256 pages ISBN 0-942061-11-X (hardcover) $29.95
ISBN 0-942061-12-8 (paperback) $17.95

Small Claims Court Without A Lawyer

by W. Kelsea Wilber, Attorney-at-Law

Small Claims Court Without A Lawyer is an invaluable guide to understanding the small claims system. It allows you to file a claim and get a judgement quickly and ecomomically, without an attorney's assistance or fee. Written in clear, uncomplicated language, this useful new book includes details about each state's small claims court system, so that wherever you live you can use it to successfully file a claim and see that claim through to a judgement.

224 pages   ISBN 0-942061-32-2 (paperback) $18.95

Also available in the Small Business Sourcebooks series:
• *Your First Business Plan* • *How to Get a Loan or Line of Credit for Your Business*
• *How to Market Your Business* • *Smart Hiring for Your Business*

To order these books or any of our numerous other publications, **please contact your local bookseller,** or call Sourcebooks at 1-800-798-2475. Get a copy of our catalog by writing or faxing:

Sourcebooks Trade
A Div. of Sourcebooks, Inc.
P.O. Box 372
Naperville, IL 60566
(708) 961-2161
FAX: 708-961-2168

Thank you for your interest in our publications.